LIVING THE
LETTERS
Philippians

A NavStudy Featuring

OUR GUARANTEE TO YOU

We believe so strongly in the message of our books that we are making this quality guarantee to you. If for any reason you are disappointed with the content of this book, return the title page to us with your name and address and we will refund to you the list price of the book. To help us serve you better, please briefly describe why you were disappointed. Mail your refund request to: NavPress, P.O. Box 35002, Colorado Springs, CO 80935.

The Navigators is an international Christian organization. Our mission is to advance the gospel of Jesus and His kingdom into the nations through spiritual generations of laborers living and discipling among the lost. We see a vital movement of the gospel, fueled by prevailing prayer, flowing freely through relational networks and out into the nations where workers for the kingdom are next door to everywhere.

NavPress is the publishing ministry of The Navigators. The mission of NavPress is to reach, disciple, and equip people to know Christ and make Him known by publishing life-related materials that are biblically rooted and culturally relevant. Our vision is to stimulate spiritual transformation through every product we publish.

ISBN-13: 978-1-60006-161-5
ISBN-10: 1-60006-161-3

Cover design by Disciple Design
Cover photo by Phillip Parker
Creative Team: Terry Behimer, Brad Lewis, Cara Iverson, Kathy Mosier, Arvid Wallen, Pat Reinheimer

Written and compiled by John Blase

Some of the anecdotal illustrations in this book are true to life and are included with the permission of the persons involved. All other illustrations are composites of real situations, and any resemblance to people living or dead is coincidental.

Excerpt on pages 72–73 is reprinted with the permission of Simon & Schuster Adult Publishing Group from *The Different Drum* by M. Scott Peck. Copyright © 1987 by M. Scott Peck, MD, PC.

All Scripture quotations in this publication are taken from *THE MESSAGE* (MSG). Copyright © 1993, 1994, 1995, 1996, 2000, 2001, 2002, 2005. Used by permission of NavPress Publishing Group.

Printed in the United States of America

1 2 3 4 5 6 7 8 9 10 / 10 09 08 07

FOR A FREE CATALOG OF NAVPRESS BOOKS & BIBLE STUDIES,
CALL 1-800-366-7788 (USA) OR 1-800-839-4769 (CANADA).

CONTENTS

ABOUT THE
LIVING THE LETTERS
SERIES

Letters take time to write, usually much more time
than talk. They require a certain level of artfulness and
thoughtfulness in expression. Then they remain, to be reread,
perhaps to be stored away for another day of reading, or
even to be encountered some distant time by a future,
unknown eavesdropper. All of these aspects of the letter
invite soulfulness: rereading is a form of reflective meditation;
keeping letters honors memory and not only daily living;
and speaking to a reader not yet present in this life
respects the soul's eternal nature.

— THOMAS MOORE, *SOUL MATES*

This isn't your typical Bible study. You won't find any blanks to fill in, questions with obvious answers, or maps of Paul's missionary journeys.

So what is *it?* That's a good question. Think of this book as an opportunity. It's a chance to allow God's Spirit to speak to you in a way that he's done for centuries — through letters.

Unfortunately, we live in a time when many consider e-mail a form of letter writing. Every once in a while, it might be. But usually it's not. Think about it: E-mail is often written quickly and absentmindedly. How many times have you clicked *send* and then thought, "Oh, no!"

As Moore points out in the above quote, letter writing takes time. Letter reading does too. So you can view this as an opportunity to add time to your day, or at least to spend what time you have in a worthy manner.

This collection of paper and ink takes Paul's letter to the Philippians and surrounds it with letters and journal entries from others in history who seemed to be trying to invite some of the same *reflective meditation*. Please understand that this isn't a subtle attempt to equate a letter or journal entry of Samuel Rutherford with the divinely inspired letter written by Paul. If anything, it's an attempt to underscore the timeless quality of God's correspondence with humanity—and to be aware of God speaking in a letter written by Anne Lamott or your Uncle Jasper.

Briefly, each lesson includes an entry from Paul's letter to the Philippians (using Eugene Peterson's *The Message*), followed by several other "letters" and a poem from contemporary writers. The challenge is to read and reread these letters. Come back and read them again days or weeks later. Questions and statements along the way will challenge you to engage the words on the page, prodding your heart, mind, soul, and strength. Yet don't approach any of this quickly or absentmindedly; rather, aim to live over and over again what you read and learn.

In so doing, might your life resemble something meditative, memorable, and eternal. *Live the letters.*

HOW TO APPROACH
LIVING THE LETTERS

This NavStudy is meant to be completed on your own and in a small group. You'll want to line up your reflection group (or whatever you want to call it) ahead of time. A group of four to six is optimal—any larger, and one or more members will likely be shut out of discussions. Your group can also be as small as two. Each person will need his or her own copy of this book.

Lessons follow the rhythm of *lectio divina*, the ancient practice of *divine reading*. The four movements are the ingredients of a spiritual frame of mind: (1) *Read*—the recitation of a short text of Scripture; (2) *Think*—an effort to wrestle with the meaning of a passage and make it personally relevant; (3) *Pray*—responding to the text and asking for God's grace in doing so; and (4) *Live*—experiencing God's love and his will for you. Divine reading has also been described in this way: Reading lies on the surface, thinking moves to the inner substance, praying involves voicing the desire, and living is the experience.

For each lesson in this book, use the four movements as follows:

1. *Read* the Scripture passage and the other readings in each section. Let them soak in. Saturate your heart, mind, soul, and strength. Reread if necessary. There's no blue ribbon for finishing quickly. Make notes in the white space on the page. If you like journaling, think of this as a space to journal.

2. *Think* about what you read. Take your time and respond to the questions provided. In addition to the questions, always ask, "What does this mean?" and "Why does this matter?" about the readings. Use your reflections to generate discussion with the other people in your group. Allow the experience of others to broaden your wisdom. You'll definitely be stretched—called on to evaluate what you've discovered

and asked to make practical sense of it. In community, this stretching can often be painful and sometimes even embarrassing. However, your willingness to be transparent—your openness to the possibility of personal growth—will reap great rewards.

3. *Pray.* That sounds so easy, doesn't it? But we all know it's not. In each lesson, read the poem provided and let God's Spirit cause words and phrases to stand out and be combined with the thoughts from the readings. Then allow that combination to be your prayer. It won't sound like a regular prayer; in fact, let this time expand your usual practice of prayer. At times, you might not be able to voice your thoughts aloud. Remember, the Spirit intercedes for us, interpreting even our "groans" to the Father.

4. *Live. Live* as in rhymes with *give.* How can you live out the thoughts, feelings, emotions, truths, challenges, and confessions you've experienced in the lesson? Each lesson will encourage you to write a letter to yourself. When your group gets together, talk over these letters. Commit to living out what you express in your letter, and ask your small group to hold you accountable with prayer and support.

TIPS FOR SMALL GROUPS

After going through each week's lesson on your own, sit down with a few other people and go deeper. Here are a few thoughts on how to make the most of that time.

Set ground rules. You don't need many. Here are two:

First, you'll want to commit, as a group, to see this through to completion. Significant personal growth happens when group members spend enough time together to really get to know each other. It doesn't have to be every week, but you do need to establish some element of consistency to your time together.

Second, agree together that everyone's story is important. Time is probably the most valuable commodity today, so if you have just an hour to spend together, do your best to give each person ample time to express concerns, pass along insights, and feel like a participating member of the group. Small-group discussions aren't monologues; however, a one-person-dominated discussion isn't always a bad thing either. Not only is your role in a small group to explore and expand your own understanding, it's also to support one another. If one group member truly needs more of the floor, give it to that person. There will be times when the needs of the one outweigh the needs of the many. Use good judgment and allow extra space when needed; *your* time might be the next time your group meets.

Meet regularly. Choose a time and place, and stick to it. Don't be surprised if this becomes a struggle. Go into this study with that expectation and push through it.

Let God lead. Each time you get together, guess who else is in the room? That's right—God. Be sensitive to how he is leading. Does your time need to be structured? If so, following the book's structure is a good idea. Does the time need breathing room instead? Then take a breath, step back, and see what God does.

Talk openly. You'll all be a little tentative at first. You're not a bad person if you're hesitant to unpack all your *stuff* in front of friends or new acquaintances. Maybe you're just a little skeptical about the value of revealing to others the deepest parts of who you are. Maybe you're simply too afraid of what those revelations might sound or look like. Discomfort isn't the goal; rather, the goal is a safe place to share and be. But don't neglect what brings you to this place—the desire to be known and find meaning for your life. And don't forget that God brings you to this place; you're not a part of your group by chance. Stretch yourself. Dip your feet in the water of honest discussion. Healing can often be found there.

Stay on task. Do you know what TMI is? Too much information. Don't spill unnecessary stuff. Talk-show transparency does little more than bolster ratings and reveal a lack of preparation. If structure isn't your group's strength, then try this approach: Spend a few minutes sharing general comments about the study, and then take each question and give everyone in the group a chance to respond.

While you're listening to others, write down thoughts that their words prompt within you. When you get to the Pray section, listen to each other read prayers aloud. Finally, give time to each person's Live section. What did each of you experience in writing a letter to yourself?

Follow up. Don't let the life application drift away without further action. Be accountable to each other and refer to previous lessons' Live sections often. Take time at the beginning of your group's meeting to review and see how you're doing. Pray for each other between times you get together. Call group members who God brings to your mind and simply ask, "How ya doin'?"

LETTER 1
FRIENDS

"Every time you cross my mind, I break out
in exclamations of thanks to God."

(PHILIPPIANS 1:3)

Before You Begin

Take just a few moments to still your heart and mind.
Remember, God desires to speak to *you* in these
moments.

> GOD *made my life complete*
> *when I placed all the pieces before him.*
>
> PSALM 18:20

READ

Philippians 1:3-8

Every time you cross my mind, I break out in exclamations of thanks to God. Each exclamation is a trigger to prayer. I find myself praying for you with a glad heart. I am so pleased that you have continued on in this with us, believing and proclaiming God's Message, from the day you heard it right up to the present. There has never been the slightest doubt in my mind that the God who started this great work in you would keep at it and bring it to a flourishing finish on the very day Christ Jesus appears.

It's not at all fanciful for me to think this way about you. My prayers and hopes have deep roots in reality. You have, after all, stuck with me all the way from the time I was thrown in jail, put on trial, and came out of it in one piece. All along you have experienced with me the most generous help from God. He knows how much I love and miss you these days. Sometimes I think I feel as strongly about you as Christ does!

THINK   "I took all this in and thought it through, inside and out." (Ecclesiastes 9:1)

- Paul indicates that when people he knows cross his mind, he prays for them—immediately. Is this concept familiar or foreign to you? If familiar, how do you pray for the people who come to mind? Share your ideas with your group. If this concept is foreign to you, try it for a day: As individuals cross your mind, just say a short prayer for them.
- Who has stuck with you so far in life? Take a few moments and thank God for these true friends.
- Just think, you might be the *only* person praying for a certain family member, friend, pastor, or college buddy today. This isn't a slight thing.

THINK (continued)

READ

From *Essays* by Ralph Waldo Emerson[1]

Friendship

There are two elements that go to the composition of friendship, each so sovereign, that I can detect no superiority in either, no reason why either should be first named. One is Truth. A friend is a person with whom I may be sincere. Before him, I may think aloud. I am arrived at last in the presence of a man so real and equal that I may drop even those undermost garments of dissimulation, courtesy, and second thought, which men never put off, and may deal with him with the simplicity and wholeness, with which one chemical atom meets another. Sincerity is the luxury allowed, like diadems and authority, only to the highest rank, *that* being permitted to speak truth, as having none above it to court or conform unto. . . .

The other element of friendship is Tenderness. We are holden to men by every sort of tie, by blood, by pride, by fear, by hope, by lucre, by lust, by hate, by admiration, by every circumstance and badge and trifle, but we can scarce believe that so much character can subsist in another as to draw us by love. Can another be so blessed, and we so pure, that we can offer him tenderness? When a man becomes dear to me, I have touched the goal of fortune.

THINK "I took all this in and thought it through, inside and out." (Ecclesiastes 9:1)

- Emerson chooses truth and tenderness as elements that comprise friendship. Do you think he's close?
- Stay with Emerson's choices for a moment. *Truth*: Do you have someone in your life who allows you—even encourages you—to think out loud? *Tenderness*: Who do you offer tenderness to? Who offers it to you?
- What other words would you use to describe the essence of friendship? Why?

THINK (continued)

READ

From *Soul Mates* by Thomas Moore[2]

A Vessel of Soul Making

In addition to whole worlds of imagination, friendship offers the soul intimacy and relatedness. Many parts of life go along fine without intimate connections. Work doesn't necessarily ask for intimate relationships, and it is possible for political and social life to be carried out without intimacy, too. But without intimacy, soul goes starving, for the closeness provided by intimate relationships fulfills the soul's very nature. Family, home, marriage, hometown, memories, personal and family stories—each gives the soul the containment it requires. Jung described the ideal setting of soul-work as an alchemical *vas*, a glass vessel in which all the stuff of the soul could be contained. Friendship is one such vessel, keeping the soul stuff together where it can go through its operations and processes. In times of emotional struggle, our first recourse might be to talk with friends, for we know that our most difficult material is safe with a friend, and that the friendship can hold our thoughts and feelings, no matter how painful or unusual, as we sift through them and watch them unfold.

THINK   "I took all this in and thought it through, inside and out." (Ecclesiastes 9:1)

* The word *soul* often seems vague or intangible—that's fair. Yet Moore might be on to something when it comes to the intimacy and depth of friendship. What words or phrases resonated with you? Why?
* Look at the list of relationships Moore provides: family, home, marriage, hometown, memories, personal and family stories. In which of these areas (or others) do you find yourself sharing "soul stuff"? Why do you think you gravitate toward that relationship for intimacy and depth? What

qualities exist in that relationship that help make soul-stuff tangible, clear, and definite?

READ

From *A Prayer for Owen Meany* by John Irving[3]

The Foul Ball

(When the narrator speaks of Owen causing his mother's death, he is referring to Owen playing in a baseball game and hitting a foul ball that struck the narrator's mother in the left temple and killed her instantly.)

I am doomed to remember a boy with a wrecked voice—not because of his voice, or because he was the smallest person I ever knew, or even because he was the instrument of my mother's death, but because he is the reason I believe in God; I am a Christian because of Owen Meany. I make no claims to have a life in Christ, or with Christ—and certainly not *for* Christ, which I've heard some zealots claim. I'm not very sophisticated in my knowledge of the Old Testament, and I've not read the New Testament since my Sunday school days, except for those passages that I hear read aloud to me when I go to church. . . .

I've always been a pretty regular churchgoer. I used to be a Congregationalist. . . . Then I became an Anglican; the Anglican Church of Canada has been my church—ever since I left the United States, about twenty years ago. . . .

I am an Anglican now, and I shall die an Anglican. But I skip a Sunday service now and then; I make no claims to be especially pious; I have a church-rummage faith—the kind that needs patching up every weekend. What faith I have I owe to Owen Meany, a boy I grew up with. It is Owen who made me a believer.

THINK   "I took all this in and thought it through, inside and out." (Ecclesiastes 9:1)

- Think about what you've just read in terms of friendship. What comes to mind about the relationship between friendship and faith? What about your own faith—who do you owe that to? Of course, God drew you to him, but who is the flesh-and-blood human being he used in that process?

Who is your Owen Meany (you might name more than one person)?

- Owen Meany was an instrument of great pain in the narrator's life, causing the death of his mother. What people have contributed to your faith through pain, suffering, or heartache?
- Have you thanked God for them? If not, don't pretend to be thankful. It might take time to see it, but tuck away this little truth: God uses all of it to grow your faith.

READ

From *Wild at Heart* by John Eldredge[4]

The Strategy

Don't even think about going into battle alone. Don't even try to take the masculine journey without at least one man by your side. Yes, there are times a man must face the battle alone, in the wee hours of the morn, and fight with all he's got. But don't make that a lifestyle of isolation. This may be our weakest point, as David Smith points out in *The Friendless American Male*: "One serious problem is the friendless condition of the average American male. Men find it hard to accept that they need the fellowship of other men." Thanks to the men's movement the church understands now that a man needs other men, but what we've offered is another two-dimensional solution: "Accountability" groups or partners. Ugh. That sounds so old covenant: "You're really a fool and you're just waiting to rush into sin, so we'd better post a guard by you to keep you in line."

We don't need accountability groups; we need fellow warriors, someone to fight alongside, someone to watch our back. A young man just stopped me on the street to say, "I feel surrounded by enemies and I'm all alone."

THINK "I took all this in and thought it through, inside and out." (Ecclesiastes 9:1)

- Do you think that Eldredge hits a bull's-eye, or is this just masculine ranting?
- While Eldredge clearly writes to men, contemporary culture can make friendships tough for everyone. In that light, choose a word or phrase to describe what his words stir in you. Does anything he says scare you?
- Why do you think friendship is so difficult? Have you experienced the "accountability" type of friendship Eldredge describes? How did that go?

THINK (continued)

PRAY

Slowly read the following poem a couple of times. What speaks to you? Ask God to bring a word or phrase to the surface. Then allow that word or phrase to begin your prayer. It might seem awkward at first. Fine, let it be awkward. But stick with it.

You Darkness

You darkness from which I come,
I love you more than all the fires
that fence out the world,
for the fire makes a circle
for everyone
so that no one sees you anymore.

But darkness holds it all:
the shape and the flame,
the animal and myself,
how it holds them,
all powers, all sight—
and it is possible: its great strength
is breaking into my body.
I have faith in the night.

—RANIER MARIA RILKE[5]

LIVE

These words from Rilke serve as a reminder of this section's theme—*friends*:

> You darkness from which I come,
> I love you more than all the fires
> that fence out the world.

You've read from the journal entries, letters, and poems of others. Now it's your turn. What does God want you to live when it comes to *friends*? Use the space below to write a letter to yourself. You might want to date the letter so you can reflect later where you were and what was going on in your life regarding *friends*.

Date _____

Dear _____

PRAYER

"So this is my prayer: that your love will flourish
and that you will not only love much but well."

(P‍HILIPPIANS 1:9)

Before You Begin

Take just a few moments to still your heart and mind.
Remember, God desires to speak to *you* in these
moments.

> *All we are and have we owe to G‍OD,*
> *Holy God of Israel, our King!*

PSALM 89:18

READ

Philippians 1:9-11

> So this is my prayer: that your love will flourish and that you will not only love much but well. Learn to love appropriately. You need to use your head and test your feelings so that your love is sincere and intelligent, not sentimental gush. Live a lover's life, circumspect and exemplary, a life Jesus will be proud of: bountiful in fruits from the soul, making Jesus Christ attractive to all, getting everyone involved in the glory and praise of God.

THINK

"I took all this in and thought it through, inside and out." (Ecclesiastes 9:1)

- Let's be honest. Most of us tend to critique prayers: "That was a great prayer, Bruce!" "I hope they don't ask Sharon to pray—ever again!" So critique Paul's prayer. Grade it on an A-to-F scale, and explain why you give it that grade.
- What line from this prayer stands out as one you hope someone will pray for you?
- *Learn to love appropriately. . . . Live a lover's life.* Add to these phrases in your own words. What do you think they mean?

READ

From *Messy Spirituality* by Michael Yaconelli[1]

Incompetence

One Sunday morning, Gary, a new Christian in our church, offered to read the Scripture for the day, which was the second chapter of Acts. During the worship service, I could see him in the front row, Bible in hand, checking the bulletin to make sure he wouldn't miss his moment. When the time came, Gary stood in front of the congregation and thumbed through his Bible, searching for the book of Acts . . . and searching . . . and searching. Finally, after two awkward minutes, he turned around and said sheepishly, "Uh, I can find the first book of Acts, but where is the second book of Acts?" Everyone laughed and someone graciously led him to the second *chapter* of the only book of Acts in the Bible. Luckily, our church is a church which expects incompetence.

Jesus responds to desire. Which is why he responded to people who interrupted him, yelled at him, touched him, screamed obscenities at him, barged in on him, crashed through ceilings to get to him. *Jesus cares more about desire than about competence*.

My hunch is most of you reading this book feel incompetent *and* you can't let go of Jesus. Jesus sees right through your incompetence into a heart longing for him.

THINK   "I took all this in and thought it through, inside and out." (Ecclesiastes 9:1)

- Do you believe Yaconelli's statement that "Jesus cares more about desire than about competence"? Or would you switch that around ("Jesus cares more about competence than about desire")? What in your own life reflects your answer?
- Look back at Paul's prayer from Philippians 1:9-11. Do you think he was praying for desire or competence on the part of his friends? Why?

- How do you pray for your friends—for them to be competent when it comes to their faith, or for them to desire to grow in their faith?

READ

From *A Good Man Is Hard to Find* by Flannery O'Connor[2]

Good Country People

(The girl in this passage, Hulga, is a highly educated atheist with a wooden leg. The boy, Manley Pointer, had come to Hulga's house selling Bibles door-to-door. In this scene, Hulga and Manley are having a picnic; Manley is making sexual advances on Hulga in the loft of a barn.)

The girl at first did not return any of the kisses but presently she began to and after she had put several on his cheek, she reached his lips and remained there, kissing him again and again as if she were trying to draw all the breath out of him. His breath was clear and sweet like a child's and the kisses were sticky like a child's. He mumbled about loving her and about knowing when he first seen her that he loved her, but the mumbling was like the sleepy fretting of a child being put to sleep by his mother. Her mind, throughout this, never stopped or lost itself for a second to her feelings. "You ain't said you loved me none," he whispered finally, pulling back from her. "You got to say that." . . .

"In a sense," she began, "if you use the word loosely, you might say that. But it's not a word I use. I don't have illusions. I'm one of those people who see *through* to nothing."

The boy was frowning. "You got to say it. I said it and you got to say it," he said.

The girl looked at him almost tenderly. "You poor baby," she murmured. "It's just as well you don't understand," and she pulled him by the neck, face-down, against her. "We are all damned," she said, "but some of us have taken off our blindfolds and see that there's nothing to see. It's a kind of salvation."

THINK   "I took all this in and thought it through, inside and out." (Ecclesiastes 9:1)

- Have you ever heard the saying, "Listen to your head, not your heart"? What do you think Hulga listened to in this scene?

- Reflect on Hulga's words: "We are all damned, but some of us have taken off our blindfolds and see that there's nothing to see." What feelings do these words stir in you? Do you pity her, agree with her, feel anger toward her, or something else? Explain.
- Would you consider this the "sentimental gush" that Paul prays against in his prayer in Philippians 1:9-11? Why or why not?

READ

From *Leaving Church* by Barbara Brown Taylor[3]

Six

(Taylor describes her pastoral experiences as pastor of
Grace-Calvary Episcopal Church.)

One local mother-and-daughter team had been coming to
Grace-Calvary for money since long before I arrived. I never
knew if they were churchgoers themselves, but they knew their
way around the county churches better than the Chamber of
Commerce did. The grown daughter was allegedly diabetic, and
the elderly mother routinely called for things that were not avail-
able from the community food bank, such as sugar-free chewing
gum, cookies, cakes, candy, canned fruit, fruit juices, soft drinks,
pudding mixes, ice cream, and pancake syrup.

Every couple of months these two did something that put
them on probation at the food bank, which meant that they really
did run short on staples from time to time. When I believed that
such a time had come, I bought them some groceries, which
kept me near the top of the mother's calling list. Even when I
said no, she took this not as discouragement but as a challenge
to try harder.

"Martha is sitting on the toilet and we are out of toilet paper,"
she told me on the telephone one afternoon. "If I came over
right now, could you write me a check to the grocery store so she
can get up?"

THINK   "I took all this in and thought it through, inside and
out." (Ecclesiastes 9:1)

• In Philippians 1:9-11, Paul prayed, "You need to use your
head and test your feelings." If you'd been in Taylor's shoes
when this woman called, what would you have done?
• If this mother-daughter team approached you again and
again, do you think an intelligent love would help them?
What do you think that would look like?

- Have you ever been in a situation like Taylor's? How did you respond to the person asking for help? What about the mother or daughter's position? Did someone give you some money or groceries or toilet paper so you could "get up"? Explain.

READ

From "Over the Top" by Ed Douglas[4]

Return to Thin Air

(Dawa Sherpa and Phurbu Temba, Nepalese Sherpas, are assisting thirty-six-year-old Burcak Pocan down the face of Mt. Everest. She was to be the first Turkish woman to reach the top, but in her bid for the summit she lost consciousness at 28,215 feet.)

For the next three hours, Dawa and Temba helped Pocan down the rocky spine to the bottom of the First Step. . . . Then something caught Dawa's eye. He expected to come across one dead body here: an Indian climber, presumably Tsewang Paljor, who lay curled under an overhang, a victim of exposure in the storm that hit Everest on May 10, 1996. . . . Paljor's plight had been noticed by two Japanese climbers, but they'd trudged past to snag the summit, leaving him to become a macabre landmark now known simply as Green Boots.

This morning, however, Dawa saw two bodies where only Green Boots should have been, the second tucked against the corpse's feet. "I say to my friend, 'This looks like new body, man,'" Dawa told me. "And my friend, he say, 'No, this one die long time ago.' And I say, 'No, no, he is another body, a new body.'". . .

The man was David Sharp, a 34-year-old British climber scaling Everest alone. . . . He'd chosen to climb without a guide or Sherpas . . . he didn't even have a radio to call for help.

Dawa said Sharp's condition was shocking: "Legs just like wood. Face already gone. Black, black. . . . We feel very bad, but we can do nothing there," Dawa told me. "It was very hard." . . . The Sherpas agreed to leave Sharp and continue on.

THINK   "I took all this in and thought it through, inside and out." (Ecclesiastes 9:1)

- What are your first reactions to this passage? You might be wondering how it could possibly relate to prayer—what are your thoughts?

- Of course, no one knows what he or she would do at 28,000 feet, under extreme circumstances. But how do the following phrases from Paul's prayer in Philippians 1:9-11 stand against this excerpt: "not only love much but well," "circumspect and exemplary," "getting everyone involved in the glory and praise of God"?

PRAY

Slowly read the following poem a couple of times. What speaks to you? Ask God to bring a word or phrase to the surface. Then allow that word or phrase to begin your prayer. It might seem awkward at first. Fine, let it be awkward. But stick with it.

The Summer Day

Who made the world?
Who made the swan, and the black bear?
Who made the grasshopper?
This grasshopper, I mean—
the one who has flung herself out of the grass,
the one who is eating sugar out of my hand,
who is moving her jaws back and forth instead of up and down—
who is gazing around with her enormous and complicated eyes.
Now she lifts her pale forearms and thoroughly washes her face.
Now she snaps her wings open, and floats away.
I don't know exactly what a prayer is.
I do know how to pay attention, how to fall down
into the grass, how to kneel down in the grass,
how to be idle and blessed, how to stroll through the fields,
which is what I have been doing all day.
Tell me, what else should I have done?
Doesn't everything die at last, and too soon?
Tell me, what is it you plan to do
with your one wild and precious life?

— MARY OLIVER[5]

LIVE

These words from Oliver serve as a reminder of this section's theme—*prayer*:

> Tell me, what is it you plan to do
> with your one wild and precious life?

You've read from the journal entries, letters, and poems of others. Now it's your turn. What does God want you to live when it comes to *prayer*? Use the space below to write a letter to yourself. You might want to date the letter so you can reflect later where you were and what was going on in your life regarding *prayer.*

Date _____

Dear _____

PROCLAMATION

"Every time one of them opens his mouth,
Christ is proclaimed."
(PHILIPPIANS 1:19)

Before You Begin

Take just a few moments to still your heart and mind.
Remember, God desires to speak to *you* in these
moments.

> *I'll write the book on your righteousness,*
> *talk up your salvation the livelong day.*
> PSALM 71:15

READ

Philippians 1:15-21

It's true that some here preach Christ because with me out of the way, they think they'll step right into the spotlight. But the others do it with the best heart in the world. One group is motivated by pure love, knowing that I am here defending the Message, wanting to help. The others, now that I'm out of the picture, are merely greedy, hoping to get something out of it for themselves. Their motives are bad. They see me as their competition, and so the worse it goes for me, the better—they think—for them.

So how am I to respond? I've decided that I really don't care about their motives, whether mixed, bad, or indifferent. Every time one of them opens his mouth, Christ is proclaimed, so I just cheer them on!

And I'm going to keep that celebration going because I know how it's going to turn out. Through your faithful prayers and the generous response of the Spirit of Jesus Christ, everything he wants to do in and through me will be done. I can hardly wait to continue on my course. I don't expect to be embarrassed in the least. On the contrary, everything happening to me in this jail only serves to make Christ more accurately known, regardless of whether I live or die. They didn't shut me up; they gave me a pulpit! Alive, I'm Christ's messenger; dead, I'm his bounty. Life versus even more life! I can't lose.

THINK   "I took all this in and thought it through, inside and out." (Ecclesiastes 9:1)

- Essentially, *proclaim* and *preach* are synonyms. Can you think of anyone, aside from the TV evangelists with funny hair, who proclaims or preaches the gospel without a pure motive? From what you've observed, what alternative motive does this individual have?

- How good do you think you are when it comes to reading motives? How often do you try to read the motives of others? Constantly, occasionally, rarely, never?
- What do you think Paul is saying about those who proclaim the gospel who have mixed or bad motives? Do you agree with him? Why or why not?

READ

From *Reclaiming God's Original Intent for the Church* by Wes Roberts and Glenn Marshall[1]

Listening/Preaching

Much of what's spoken in preaching is true. But is it relevant to the real needs of people in the world? People have real needs in addition to their felt needs. People have a real need to hear the gospel, to see it in action, and experience it. They have a real need to commit their lives to Christ. They need to repent of sin and believe the gospel of the kingdom. They need to find their purpose in life by becoming dependent on their Creator. However, we need to listen to the people in the world so we have points of contact with them.

Have you been listening—or just preaching?

Our world holds a lot of despair, purposelessness, and hopelessness. As people chase after money, prestige, and power, they hide their problems pretty well. No one likes to talk about their problems, but they're there. . . .

If we make the intentional investment of listening to the world so that we might speak the truth in love, many in our congregations will do the same. . . . This is no easy task, but it's our calling. Remember that Jesus hung out with all types of worldly characters before he hung on a cross for us.

THINK   "I took all this in and thought it through, inside and out." (Ecclesiastes 9:1)

- Roberts and Marshall make a case for a strong connection between preaching and listening. Do you agree or disagree? Explain.
- What about you—do you follow the old adage that perhaps your mother repeated when you were a sassy teenager: "God gave you two ears and one mouth because he wants you to listen twice as much as you speak"? When it comes to

listening to people's needs, is your math somehow different?

- "Jesus hung out with all types of worldly characters before he hung on a cross for us." Think through some of the people Jesus ministered to during his earthly life. Why do you think he "hung out with all types of worldly characters"?

READ

From *The Earth Is Enough* by Harry Middleton[2]

Readings at Dusk

(Albert and Emerson are two old brothers living their days out in the
hills of northwest Arkansas. Elias Wonder is an Indian who lives on their
place. The narrator is the nephew of Albert and Emerson, sent there to
live for a time while his father is in the war. These three men are some of
the few left who believe that the earth is enough.)

I never really knew how long it had been going on. Perhaps thirty
years. Maybe more. By the time of my arrival among the old men,
the meetings between them and the good Reverend Biddle had
long since settled into an uncomplicated ritual. Biddle knew
that Albert and Emerson and Elias Wonder were well anchored
beyond whatever he might tell them, say to them, either as friend
or reverend. That didn't matter, however, because he liked them,
perhaps even admired them a little. Likewise, the old men liked
the Reverend Biddle and often felt bad that they couldn't bring
themselves to believe in the God that he believed in so totally
and unconditionally. Sometimes, I thought that perhaps they
envied him, as well.

The Reverend Biddle came to the house the last Sunday of
every month. These Sundays were always looked forward to, for
they involved a good meal, wine, hours of head conversation.
Biddle took it as his personal mission to save the old men from
hell. He had determined years before that they should be led,
willingly or not, into the magnanimous arms of righteousness.

Biddle had tired, mouselike eyes, a rounded, fleshy chin,
sunken cheeks, and a few tufts of silky gray hair on his melon-
shaped head. He was given to moping about a great deal, and
from his perpetually slumped shoulders one got the impression
that he hauled the sins of the world . . . on his aching back.

THINK "I took all this in and thought it through, inside and out." (Ecclesiastes 9:1)

- Based on the narrator's description, what do you think of the message that the good Reverend Biddle proclaimed? Think beyond his words, to his monthly visits to the old men, the way he looked, the way he "hauled the sins of the world" on his back.
- Why do you suppose the old men liked Biddle?
- How would you respond to someone who told Biddle, "You haven't gotten anywhere in thirty years; you need to move on where the needs are greater"?

READ

From *The River Why* by David James Duncan[3]

Excerpts from the God-Notebook

(The narrator refers to his father as "H2O" and his brother as "Bill Bob." The narrator describes the door-to-door evangelism experience in their household of devout fly fishermen and women.)

The door-to-door comic-book distribution is part of an activity these folk call "Witnessing"—"Witlessing," as my mother renders it. The divergent courses of action my family members took when these threat-peddlers came knocking are worth noting: H2O classified the "Witless" according to gender—the men he called "the Christian Brothers" after Ma's brandy, the women "the Weird Sisters" after the witches in Macbeth. When they offered him the comics they called "littercher"—"a term," said H2O, "the first two syllables of which approach the truth"—he would coolly misinform them that he and his family were passionately attached to the Church of England and had no use for their propaganda. . . .

Ma's technique was less articulate, more woodsy, and such a delight to Bill Bob and me that a dull rainy day would sometimes sink us to our knees to beseech Fathern Heaven or R. Lord to send along a Witless. When the knocker sounded, Ma would size up the visitor through a fisheye peephole she'd installed for such occasions. If she spotted comic books she would repair to the closet, return to the door, let it swing slowly open, and stand there—wordless, immobile and menacing—while the unfortunate caller grew cognizant of the fact that a wild, unreliable-looking woman had a double-barreled shotgun aimed at his or her knees. (Ma figured if you shot their knees you shot their ability to pray.)

THINK   "I took all this in and thought it through, inside and out." (Ecclesiastes 9:1)

- Proverbs 17:22 says, "A cheerful disposition is good for your health; gloom and doom leave you bone-tired." Did you find that Duncan's descriptions made you cheerful or full of gloom and doom? Explain.
- Have you ever had a "witlessing" experience? Whether you were the witness or the one being witnessed to, describe it as best you can.
- Even if you disagree with this style of proclaiming, how do you think it fits with what Paul writes in Philippians 1: "Every time one of them opens his mouth, Christ is proclaimed, so I just cheer them on!" (verse 19)?

READ

From *The Orphean Passages* by Walter Wangerin Jr.[4]

Death and Mourning

(This is a fictional account of Reverend Orpheus,
a white pastor in a black parish in the inner city.)

Orpheus was a pastor. He could not think of a better, more honorable thing to be. . . .

Once, while he was preaching (he stood in the aisle to preach, feeling too separated from the people by the pulpit, feeling too official underneath his God within a pulpit), he caught up a restless child in his arms and continued to speak while he rocked this child. And what did she do? She curled against his breast. She clung to his neck. And what did the people do? First they smiled; but then they dropped warm tears at the sight.

Reverend Orpheus was not surprised by their tears, though he had not intended such a reaction. Rather, he thought to himself, *The dear Lord Jesus is here. They see that, too. So their tears were his tears, because the gentle presence of Jesus always caused a joy that overflowed in tears.* He understood.

Often, thereafter, he forgot formalities and acted in a manner most familiar. Close to Jesus, close to the people: the first permitted the second; the second revealed the first.

And the consequence of both was that the people grew very close to Reverend Orpheus. They loved him much.

THINK "I took all this in and thought it through, inside and out." (Ecclesiastes 9:1)

- "Close to Jesus, close to the people." What's your reaction to Orpheus's philosophy?
- Based on Wangerin's description, what do you think of the message that Reverend Orpheus proclaimed?

- You've read about several pastors. What do you appreciate about your own pastor? Have you expressed your appreciation to him or her recently?

PRAY

Slowly read the following poem a couple of times. What speaks to you? Ask God to bring a word or phrase to the surface. Then allow that word or phrase to begin your prayer. It might seem awkward at first. Fine, let it be awkward. But stick with it.

Ash Wednesday

And pray to God to have mercy upon us
And pray that I may forget
These matters that with myself I too much discuss
Too much explain
Because I do not hope to turn again
Let these words answer
For what is done, not to be done again
May the judgment not be too heavy upon us

Because these wings are no longer wings to fly
But merely vans to beat the air
The air which is now thoroughly small and dry
Smaller and dryer than the will
Teach us to care and not to care
Teach us to sit still.

—T. S. ELIOT[5]

LIVE

These words from Eliot serve as a reminder of this section's theme—*proclamation*:

Teach us to care and not to care
Teach us to sit still.

You've read from the journal entries, letters, and poems of others. Now it's your turn. What does God want you to live when it comes to *proclamation*? Use the space below to write a letter to yourself. You might want to date the letter so you can reflect later where you were and what was going on in your life regarding *proclamation*.

Date _____

Dear _____

LETTER 4

SUFFERING

"And the suffering is as much a gift as the trusting."
(PHILIPPIANS 1:29)

Before You Begin

Take just a few moments to still your heart and mind.
Remember, God desires to speak to *you* in these
moments.

> *My sad life's dilapidated, a falling-down barn;*
> *build me up again by your Word.*
>
> PSALM 119:28

READ

Philippians 1:27-30

> Meanwhile, live in such a way that you are a credit to the Message of Christ. Let nothing in your conduct hang on whether I come or not. Your conduct must be the same whether I show up to see things for myself or hear of it from a distance. Stand united, singular in vision, contending for people's trust in the Message, the good news, not flinching or dodging in the slightest before the opposition. Your courage and unity will show them what they're up against: defeat for them, victory for you—and both because of God. There's far more to this life than trusting in Christ. There's also suffering for him. And the suffering is as much a gift as the trusting. You're involved in the same kind of struggle you saw me go through, on which you are now getting an updated report in this letter.

THINK   *"I took all this in and thought it through, inside and out."* (Ecclesiastes 9:1)

- What's your reaction to the statement, "There's far more to this life than trusting in Christ"? Why?
- When it comes to your faith, when's the last time you thought, *The suffering is as much a gift as the trusting*? Be honest—do you ever think about suffering as a gift?
- Break down that thought further. Do you accept suffering as part of your faith journey? Or do you try to avoid or escape suffering? Explain your reaction.

THINK (continued)

READ

From *When the Heart Waits* by Sue Monk Kidd[1]

Crisis as Opportunity

A minister friend of mine, who has seen countless Christians through crisis events, told me that he didn't think most Christians knew *how* to have a crisis — at least not creatively.

He started me wondering. For the most part, we do one of two things in response to a crisis. We say that it's God's will and force ourselves into an outwardly sweet acceptance, remaining unaffected at the deeper level of the spirit. People who have a crisis in this manner are generally after comfort and peace of mind.

Or we reject the crisis, fighting and railing against it until we become cynical and defeated or suffer a loss of faith. People who choose this way to have a crisis are after justice.

Yet there's a third way to have a crisis: the way of waiting. That way means creating a painfully honest and contemplative relationship with one's own depths, with God in the deep center of one's soul. People who choose this way aren't so much after peace of mind or justice as wholeness and transformation. They're after soulmaking.

If you choose this way, you find the threshold, the creative moment or epiphany, within the crisis. You discover that the stormy experience can be an agent drawing you deeper into the kingdom, separating you from the old consciousness and the clamp of the ego. It's not an easy way.

THINK   "I took all this in and thought it through, inside and out." (Ecclesiastes 9:1)

• Consider the most recent crisis in your life. Which of Kidd's three ways to deal with the crisis did you choose as your response? Explain.

- When you face a crisis, what do you usually seek: comfort and peace of mind, justice, or wholeness and transformation? Take some time to answer honestly.
- If you've ever chosen the third way—the way of waiting—describe the experience. Kidd writes, "It's not an easy way." Do you agree or disagree? Explain.

READ

From *Lament for a Son* by Nicholas Wolterstorff[2]

Suffering

(Wolterstorff's twenty-five-year-old son, Eric, was killed in a climbing
accident. This is one of the classic modern texts on grief.)

Suffering may do us good—may be a blessing, something to be
thankful for. This I have learned. . . .

Suffering is the shout of "No" by one's whole existence to
that over which one suffers—the shout of "No" by nerves and
gut and gland and heart to pain, to death, to injustice, to depres-
sion, to hunger, to humiliation, to bondage, to abandonment.
And sometimes, when the cry is intense, there emerges a radiance which elsewhere seldom appears: a glow of courage, of
love, of insight, of selflessness, of faith. In that radiance we see
best what humanity was meant to be.

That the radiance which emerges from acquaintance with
grief is a blessing to others is familiar, though perplexing: How
can we treasure the radiance while struggling against what
brought it about? How can we thank God for suffering's yield
while asking for its removal? But what I have learned is something stranger still: Suffering may be among the sufferer's bless-
ings. I think of a former colleague who, upon recovering from a
heart attack, remarked that he would not have missed it for the
life of him.

In the valley of suffering, despair and bitterness are brewed.
But there also character is made. The valley of suffering is the
vale of soulmaking.

THINK
"I took all this in and thought it through, inside and out." (Ecclesiastes 9:1)

- What words or phrases prompted you to say, "Yes"? How about, "I don't think so," or "That wouldn't work for me"? What left you wondering?
- Wolterstorff writes that suffering as good is something he has *learned*. Do you believe this must be learned patiently over time? Explain your answer.
- How would you answer Wolterstorff's question, "How can we thank God for suffering's yield while asking for its removal?"

READ

From *The Lives of Rocks* by Rick Bass[3]

The Lives of Rocks

(Bass's fictional character, Jyl, lives alone in a cabin in the mountains, and she's a cancer survivor. Her life prior to cancer was one of solid independence. Her only neighbors are a family of fundamentalist Christians. Jyl believes that their work is their religion—they are always doing something. Two of the children, Stephan and Shayna, are visiting her.)

They sat at the table, where Jyl had not had company in several months. She tried to remember the last company she'd had, and could not. The memory of it, the fact of it, seemed to get tangled in the snow falling outside the window which they sat watching.

"Mama said to ask you how you're doing," Stephan said. "If you need anything. If there's anything we can do." He peered sidelong at Jyl, evaluating, she could tell, her girth, or gauntness, to take back home to tell his mother—glancing at her and making a reading or judgment as he would in a similar glance the health of a cow or horse, or even some wild creature in the woods, one he was perhaps considering taking. "She said to ask if you're eating yet." Another glance, as if he'd been warned that the interviewee might not be trusted to give direct or even truthful answers. "She said to ask if you needed any propane. If you needed any firewood. If you needed any firewood split. If you needed any water hauled."

He said this last task so flatly, so casually and indifferently, that his practiced childish nonchalance illuminated rather than hid his distaste for the job, and again Jyl smiled, almost laughed and said, "No, I don't need any water hauled, thank you." . . .

"But you need some wood," Stephan said. A glance at the nearly empty wood box by the stove—only a few sticks of kindling. "Everybody always needs wood, and especially split wood." Another evaluation of her physique—the wasted arms, the pallor. The steady fright.

"Yes," Jyl admitted, "I could use some wood. And I've been wondering, too, what I'll do if I go out hunting, and do get an

animal down. Before my illness—my cancer—I could just gut
it and drag it home from wherever I'd shot it. But now it would
take me so many trips that the ravens and eagles and coyotes
would finish it off long before I ever got it all packed out."

Stephan nodded, as if the concern were music to his ears.
"We can help with that," he said, and she saw that already his
indoctrination was complete, that work had become his religion,
that it transcended escape and was instead merely its own pure
thing: that from early on, he and his brothers and sisters had
been poured into the vessel of it, and it would be forever after
how they were comfortable in the world. "We can take care of
that," he said. "If you get an animal, you just let us know."

THINK   "I took all this in and thought it through, inside and
out." (Ecclesiastes 9:1)

- As you look back through Bass's words, what do you like
  about Jyl? What about the children?
- In Philippians 1:29, Paul said, "The suffering is as much a gift
  as the trusting." What gifts are exchanged in this passage?
- Do you see other suffering, besides Jyl's cancer, in these
  lives? Explain.

READ

From *The Solace of Open Spaces* by Gretel Ehrlich[4]

Other Lives

(Born, raised, and schooled in California, Ehrlich went to Wyoming
on a documentary film assignment. She ended up falling in love
with the land and the people and decided to stay.)

Nineteen seventy-eight turned out to be the third worst Wyoming
winter on record. After an extreme of sixty below zero, the ther-
mometer rose to ten below and the air felt balmy. . . .

It was hard to know who suffered more—the livestock or
the ranchers who fed and cared for them. . . .

Days when the temperature never rose above zero my log
cabin felt like a forest pulled around me. . . .

Ellen Cotton, who ranches alone northeast of the Big Horns,
called me late one night: "I just don't think I can get this feeding
done by myself. This snow is so darned deep and this old team of
mine won't stand still for me when I get down to open the gates.
Could you come over and help?" . . .

I had once asked Ellen how she withstood the frustrations of
ranching alone. Because she is the granddaughter of Ralph Waldo
Emerson, I imagined she possessed unusual reserves of hardiness.
But she protested. "I don't do a very good job of it," she said mod-
estly. "I get in these hoarding moods and get mad at myself for all
the stupid things I do. Then I pick up this old kaleidoscope and
give it a whirl. See, it's impossible to keep just one thing in view. It
gives way to other things and they're all beautiful."

THINK   "I took all this in and thought it through, inside and
out." (Ecclesiastes 9:1)

* How do Ehrlich's words strike you? Do you see dismal suffering, colorful hope, or both? Explain.
* What area of your life—right now, or in the recent
  past—could be described as feeling like "an extreme of sixty
  below zero"?

- What would it take (or what did it take) for you to begin looking at suffering in a different way—to see how things give way "to other things and they're all beautiful"?

PRAY

Slowly read the following poem a couple of times. What speaks to you? Ask God to bring a word or phrase to the surface. Then allow that word or phrase to begin your prayer. It might seem awkward at first. Fine, let it be awkward. But stick with it.

Noah

They gathered around and told him not to do it,
They formed a committee and tried to take control,
They cancelled his building permit and they stole
His plans. I sometimes wonder how he got through it.
He told them wrath was coming, they would rue it,
He begged them to believe the tides would roll,
He offered them passage to his destined goal,
A new world. They were finished and he knew it.
All to no end.
     And then the rain began.
A spatter at first that barely wet the soil,
Then showers, quick rivulets lacing the town,
Then deluge universal. The old man
Arthritic from his years of scorn and toil
Leaned from the admiral's walk and watched them drown.

— ROY DANIELLS[5]

LIVE

These words from Daniells serve as a reminder of this section's theme—*suffering*:

> The old man
> Arthritic from his years of scorn and toil . . .

You've read from the journal entries, letters, and poems of others. Now it's your turn. What does God want you to live when it comes to *suffering*? Use the space below to write a letter to yourself. You might want to date the letter so you can reflect later where you were and what was going on in your life regarding *suffering*.

Date _____

Dear _____

ONE ANOTHER

"Agree with each other, love each other, be deep-spirited friends. . . . Put yourself aside, and help others get ahead."
(PHILIPPIANS 2:2,4)

Before You Begin

Take just a few moments to still your heart and mind. Remember, God desires to speak to *you* in these moments.

> *In God we'll do our very best;*
> *he'll flatten the opposition for good.*
> PSALM 60:12

READ

Philippians 2:1-8

If you've gotten anything at all out of following Christ, if his love
has made any difference in your life, if being in a community
of the Spirit means anything to you, if you have a heart, if you
care—then do me a favor: Agree with each other, love each
other, be deep-spirited friends. Don't push your way to the front;
don't sweet-talk your way to the top. Put yourself aside, and help
others get ahead. Don't be obsessed with getting your own advan-
tage. Forget yourselves long enough to lend a helping hand.

Think of yourselves the way Christ Jesus thought of himself.
He had equal status with God but didn't think so much of himself that he had to cling to the advantages of that status no matter
what. Not at all. When the time came, he set aside the privileges
of deity and took on the status of a slave, became *human*! Having
become human, he stayed human. It was an incredibly humbling
process. He didn't claim special privileges. Instead, he lived a selfless, obedient life and then died a selfless, obedient death—and
the worst kind of death at that—a crucifixion.

THINK

"I took all this in and thought it through, inside and
out." (Ecclesiastes 9:1)

- Look through this passage again. Make a list of positive qualities or behaviors Paul writes about.
- Now make a list of the negative qualities or behaviors you find.
- Look through your lists. In your own words, make a few
notes about what the qualities and behaviors mean. Which
words from each list describe you? Which words would you
like to have describe you?
- As you look at the words that describe you, what causes you
to behave that way or to have those qualities—your person-
ality, environment, upbringing, faith journey, relationships,
or something else?

THINK (continued)

READ

From *Community and Growth* by Jean Vanier[1]

Community and Cooperation

In community, collaboration must find its source in communion. It is because people care for each other and feel called to be with each other, walking towards the same goals, that they co-operate together. Co-operation without communion quickly becomes like a work camp or factory, where unity comes from an exterior reality. And there will be many tensions and strife.

Communion is based on some common inner experience of love; it is the recognition of being one body, one people, called by God to be a source of love and peace. Its fulfillment is more in silence than in words, more in celebration than in work. It is an experience of openness and trust that flows from what is innermost in a person; it is a gift of the Holy Spirit.

Community is above all a place of communion. For this reason it is necessary to give priority in daily life to those realities, symbols, meetings and celebrations that will encourage a consciousness of communion. When a community is just a place of work, it is in danger of dying.

THINK

"I took all this in and thought it through, inside and out." (Ecclesiastes 9:1)

- Vanier describes two realities of community: with communion and without communion. First, in your own words, write down what you think communion means. Now consider your experiences of community, past and present. Which of the two realities describes most of your experiences?
- If your experiences of community have more often been "with communion," reflect on the attitudes or actions that helped bring that about. Was the communion intentional, or did it just happen?

- If your experiences of community have more often been
  "without communion," what are repeating ways those
  groups have kept communion at arm's length? Do you think
  it to be simply bad timing, strange personalities, poor leadership, or something else? Explain.

READ

From *The Different Drum* by M. Scott Peck[2]

A Spirit

Community *is* a spirit—but not in the way that the familiar phrase "community spirit" is usually understood. To most of us it implies a competitive spirit, a jingoistic boosterism, such as that displayed by fans of winning football teams or the citizens of a town in which they take great pride. "Our town is better than your town" might be taken as a typical expression of community spirit.

But this understanding of the spirit of community is profoundly misleading as well as dreadfully shallow. In only one respect is it accurate. The members of a group who have achieved genuine community take pleasure—even delight—in themselves as a collective. They know they have won something together, collectively discovered something of great value, that they are "onto something." Beyond that the similarity ends. There is nothing competitive, for instance, about the spirit of true community. To the contrary, a group possessed by a spirit of competitiveness is by definition not a community. Competitiveness is always exclusive; genuine community is inclusive. If community has enemies, it has begun to lose the spirit of community—if it ever had it in the first place.

The spirit of true community is the spirit of peace. People in the early stages of a community-building workshop will frequently ask, "How will we know when we are a community?" It is a needless question. When a group enters community there is a dramatic change in spirit. And the new spirit is almost palpable. There is no mistaking it. No one who has experienced it need ever ask again, "How will we know when we are a community?" . . .

But the spirit is slippery. It does not submit itself to definition, to capture, the way material things do. So it is that a group in community does not always feel peaceful in the usual sense of the word. Its members will from time to time struggle with each other, and struggle hard. The struggle may become excited and exuberant with little, if any, room for silence. But it is a productive, not a destructive, struggle. It always moves toward consensus, because it is always a loving struggle. It takes place on a ground of love. The spirit of community is inevitably the spirit of peace and love.

THINK "I took all this in and thought it through, inside and out." (Ecclesiastes 9:1)

- Go back and read Paul's Philippians 2:1-4. Do you think Peck's words complement or contradict Paul's desire? Explain.
- Peck writes, "A productive, not a destructive, struggle . . . always moves toward consensus, because it is always a loving struggle." In your own words, define productive struggle, destructive struggle, and loving struggle.
- As you think back through the communities you've been a part of, can you recall a productive, or loving, struggle? What was the result of that struggle for you personally—growing, learning patience, learning to listen, or something else?

READ

From *Lord, Teach Us* by William Willimon and Stanley Hauerwas[3]

"Your Will Be Done, on Earth as in Heaven"

Too often, we are conditioned to think of prayer as asking God for what we want—dear God, give me this, give me that. But now, in praying that God's will be done on earth as it is in heaven, we are attempting to school ourselves to want what God wants. We receive, not what our hearts desire, but rather we become so enthralled with a vision of what God is doing on earth and in heaven, that we forget the story that the world has told us—that we have nothing better to do than to satisfy our desires.

We live in a society of omnivorous desire. Prayer can be risky in such an environment. In our culture, everything—all philosophies, psychologies, all people and things—are reduced to techniques, methods of getting what our hearts desire. Our culture is a vast supermarket of desire in which we are encouraged constantly to consume. . . .

So we lurch from this experience to that, try on this mask or that one, switch friends, grope for new thrills, buy this, drink that, all in a frantic, never-ending attempt to "Get what I want," fearful that we might miss the one experience that would really make our lives worth living.

"Getting what I want" is related to my knowledge of my real self, my imagination or lack of it, the range of my experience and wisdom.

THINK   "I took all this in and thought it through, inside and out." (Ecclesiastes 9:1)

- Willimon and Hauerwas don't mince words, do they? What's your reaction to their thoughts?
- Think about the last three months of your life. Pinpoint times and situations where you've tried to "get what you

want." You don't need to say whether you got it or not; just identify what was going on.

- As you think through these times, can you see any indications that you're not in tune with who you really are? Do the words, "'Getting what I want' is related to my knowledge of my real self, my imagination or lack of it" apply to you? Do you think your desires for this or that reveal a false self instead of a true self? Wrestle with those thoughts for a while.

READ

From *In the Name of Jesus* by Henri Nouwen[4]

From Popularity to Ministry

(Nouwen's focus is priests and ministers; however,
the truth here is applicable to anyone.)

Confession and forgiveness are the concrete forms in which
we sinful people love one another. Often I have the impression
that priests and ministers are the least-confessing people in the
Christian community. The sacrament of Confession has often
become a way to keep our own vulnerability hidden from our
community. . . .

How can priests or ministers feel really loved and cared
for when they have to hide their own sins and failings from the
people to whom they minister and run off to a distant stranger
to receive a little comfort and consolation? How can people truly
care for their shepherds and keep them faithful to their sacred
task when they do not know them and so cannot deeply love
them? I am not at all surprised that so many ministers and priests
suffer immensely from the deep emotional loneliness, frequently
feel a great need for affectivity and intimacy, and sometimes
experience a deep-seated guilt and shame in front of their own
people. Often they seem to say, "What if my people knew how I
really feel, what I think and daydream about, and where my mind
wanders when I am sitting by myself in my study?" It is precisely
the men and women who are dedicated to spiritual leadership
who are easily subject to very raw carnality. The reason for this is
that they do not know how to live the truth of the Incarnation.

THINK   "I took all this in and thought it through, inside and
out." (Ecclesiastes 9:1)

- What about you? Is confession and forgiveness a consistent
  part of your life? What about confession and forgiveness as
  heard and experienced in community?

- What about this reflection group you meet with? Do you make confession and forgiveness an integral part of this journey? No fair answering, "Well, that's not in the introduction as part of what we're supposed to do in this study." Technically, you're correct. But if you want to move closer to one another's lives (also known as "intimacy"), then confession and forgiveness are necessary parts of getting together. If confession and forgiveness haven't been part of your times together, take some time to discuss how you might change that.

PRAY

Slowly read the following poem a couple of times. What speaks to you? Ask God to bring a word or phrase to the surface. Then allow that word or phrase to begin your prayer. It might seem awkward at first. Fine, let it be awkward. Yes, this is the Lord's Prayer. But praying it, really praying it, can be awkward. Stick with it.

> Our Father in heaven,
> Reveal who you are.
> Set the world right;
> Do what's best—
>   as above, so below.
> Keep us alive with three square meals.
> Keep us forgiven with you and forgiving others.
> Keep us safe from ourselves and the Devil.
> You're in charge!
> You can do anything you want!
> You're ablaze in beauty!
>   Yes. Yes. Yes.[5]

LIVE

These words from Scripture serve as a reminder of this section's
theme—*one another*:

Keep us forgiven with you and forgiving others.

You've read from the journal entries, letters, and poems of
others. Now it's your turn. What does God want you to live when it
comes to *one another*? Use the space below to write a letter to yourself. You might want to date the letter so you can reflect later where
you were and what was going on in your life regarding *one another.*

Date _____

Dear _____

LETTER 6

THE WORLD

"Provide people with a glimpse of good living
and of the living God."

(PHILIPPIANS 2:15)

Before You Begin

Take just a few moments to still your heart and mind.
Remember, God desires to speak to *you* in these
moments.

What a wildly wonderful world, GOD!

PSALM 104:24

READ

Philippians 2:12-16

What I'm getting at, friends, is that you should simply keep on
doing what you've done from the beginning. When I was living
among you, you lived in responsive obedience. Now that I'm separated from you, keep it up. Better yet, redouble your efforts. Be
energetic in your life of salvation, reverent and sensitive before
God. That energy is *God's* energy, an energy deep within you,
God himself willing and working at what will give him the most
pleasure.

Do everything readily and cheerfully—no bickering, no
second-guessing allowed! Go out into the world uncorrupted,
a breath of fresh air in this squalid and polluted society. Provide
people with a glimpse of good living and of the living God. Carry
the light-giving Message into the night so I'll have good cause to
be proud of you on the day that Christ returns. You'll be living
proof that I didn't go to all this work for nothing.

THINK

"I took all this in and thought it through, inside and
out." (Ecclesiastes 9:1)

- Paul writes of a "squalid and polluted society." What words
  would you use to describe the society you live in?
- Can you think of any recent events that stand in contrast to
  the words you listed above?
- "Provide people with a glimpse of good living and of the
  living God." All in all, do you think Christians do a good
  job of this? Or do most simply stand back and criticize our
  "squalid and polluted society"?

THINK (continued)

READ

From *The Wisdom of the Desert* by Thomas Merton[1]

Introduction

In the fourth century A.D. the deserts of Egypt, Palestine, Arabia and Persia were peopled by a race of men who have left behind them a strange reputation. They were the first Christian hermits, who abandoned the cities of the pagan world to live in solitude. Why did they do this? The reasons were many and various, but they can all be summed up in one word as the quest for "salvation." . . .

The flight of these men to the desert was neither purely negative nor purely individualistic. They were not rebels against society. True, they were in a certain sense "anarchists," and it will do no harm to think of them in that light. They were men who did not believe in letting themselves be passively guided and ruled by a decadent state, and who believed that there was a way of getting along without slavish dependence on accepted, conventional values. . . .

What the Fathers sought most of all was their own true self, in Christ. And in order to do this, they had to reject completely the false, formal self, fabricated under social compulsion in "the world."

THINK
"I took all this in and thought it through, inside and out." (Ecclesiastes 9:1)

- Does this "Desert Father" path sound attractive to you some days? Why or why not?
- Do you think you can live a "Desert Father" lifestyle right where you are? How? Explain.
- Do you think it's possible to live in this society and not be influenced or controlled by the decadent culture? Be as specific as you can.

LETTER 6 / 85

THINK (continued)

READ

From *New Seeds of Contemplation* by Thomas Merton[2]

Solitude Is Not Separation

Some men have perhaps become hermits with the thought that sanctity could only be attained by escape from other men. But the only justification for a life of deliberate solitude is the conviction that it will help you to love not only God but also other men. If you go into the desert merely to get away from people you dislike, you will find neither peace nor solitude. . . .

The need for true solitude is a complex and dangerous thing, but it is a real need. It is all the more real today when the collectivity tends more and more to swallow up the person in its shapeless and faceless mass. The temptation of our day is to equate "love" and "conformity"—passive subservience to the mass-mind or to the organization. This temptation is only strengthened by futile rebellion on the part of eccentrics who want to be madly and notably different and who thereby create for themselves only a new kind of dullness—a dullness that is erratic instead of predictable. . . .

Without a certain element of solitude there can be no compassion because when a man is lost in the wheels of a social machine he is no longer aware of human needs as a matter of personal responsibility. One can escape from men by plunging into the midst of a crowd!

Go into the desert not to escape other men but in order to find them in God.

THINK   "I took all this in and thought it through, inside and out." (Ecclesiastes 9:1)

- What does *solitude* mean to you? Don't try to come up with a dictionary definition; just put it into your own words.
- Reread Paul's words in Philippians 2:12-16. Where would solitude fit into what he writes?

- While nuances always exist, try to answer the following as an "either/or" question. Do you believe the current Christian atmosphere is varied and creative, or dull and conformist? Explain.

READ

From *The Monastic Impulse* by Walter Capps[3]

Discernment

(A group of students are visiting a monastery, when one of them asks the abbot, "Father, if you had it to do over again, would you?")

The abbot heard the question, but it was some time before the answer came.

"Yes, I think so," he said. . . .

In words carefully selected and barely audible, he continued, "Yes, if I had to do it over again, I would try to change one important component. . . . I wish I had been more generous." . . .

When he was younger, a student like them, he thought that being critical was an art to be cultivated and most highly prized. This is what his courses of study had led him to conclude. "All of us," he summarized, "have been taught to be critical.". . .

Now that he is older, however, he knows that although he might have written five books of criticism of the nation . . . and on a subject he knows even more about, the Church, he might have written ten books of criticism . . . very little distinctive talent would have been required for this. . . . All that is needed is a careful enunciation of the capacity modern human beings utilize most naturally and have cultivated most highly.

"Generosity, on the other hand, is a lost art," he continued. Trained by the dictates of the critical temper, we have lost touch with generosity. We no longer know what it means, intends, involves. We have only an underdeveloped appreciation of what it is capable of.

THINK   "I took all this in and thought it through, inside and out." (Ecclesiastes 9:1)

* Take some time to reflect as you answer. If you had your life up to this point to do over again, what one important component or quality would you try to change? Why?

- In Philippians 2:16, Paul writes that those who follow Christ "carry the light-giving Message." Yet the abbot charges that "all of us have been taught to be critical." How do you reconcile these two thoughts? Which description rings more true in your experience?

READ

From *Meditations* by Thomas Moore[4]

Utopia

St. Thomas Moore wrote in Utopia: What you cannot turn to good you must make as little bad as you can.

He lived a vibrant family life, enjoyed political power, and always sought the monastic spirit. A man for all seasons, his life was a zodiac of attachments and devotedness. In particular he followed an ancient humanist insight: the life of the spirit flourishes in combination with a subtle, reserved, carefully focused life of pleasure.

If you aim at a life of spiritual purity, then you, more than most, must cultivate honest worldly pleasures.

THINK   "I took all this in and thought it through, inside and out." (Ecclesiastes 9:1)

- "If you aim at a life of spiritual purity, then you, more than most, must cultivate honest worldly pleasures." How do you react to this thought?
- What does your life of pleasure look, sound, or taste like? Think less about revealing the pleasure itself, and focus more on describing what prompts you to seek it.
- How do you reconcile your worldly pleasures with your journey of faith? Do you compartmentalize, feel guilty, justify, or something else?

PRAY

Slowly read the following poem a couple of times. What speaks to you? Ask God to bring a word or phrase to the surface. Then allow that word or phrase to begin your prayer. It might seem awkward at first. Fine, let it be awkward. But stick with it.

> O, tell us, poet, what do you do?
>   I praise.
> But the deadly and the violent days,
> how do you undergo them, take them in?
>   I praise.
> But the namelessness—how do you raise
> that, invoke the unnameable?
>   I praise.
> What right have you, through every phase,
> in every mask, to remain true?
>   I praise.
> —and that both stillness and the wild affray
> know you, like star and storm?
>   Because I praise.
>
> —RANIER MARIA RILKE[5]

LIVE

These words from Rilke serve as a reminder of this section's
theme—*the world*:

Because I praise.

You've read from the journal entries, letters, and poems of
others. Now it's your turn. What does God want you to live when it
comes to *the world*? Use the space below to write a letter to yourself.
You might want to date the letter so you can reflect later where you
were and what was going on in your life regarding *the world*.

Date _____

Dear _____

"Oh, how that will do my heart good!"
(Philippians 2:20)

Before You Begin

Take just a few moments to still your heart and mind. Remember, God desires to speak to *you* in these moments.

Hallelujah! Sing to God a brand-new song,
praise him in the company of all who love him.

PSALM 149:1

READ

Philippians 2:19-30

I plan (according to Jesus' plan) to send Timothy to you very soon so he can bring back all the news of you he can gather. Oh, how that will do my heart good! I have no one quite like Timothy. He is loyal, and genuinely concerned for you. Most people around here are looking out for themselves, with little concern for the things of Jesus. But you know yourselves that Timothy's the real thing. He's been a devoted son to me as together we've delivered the Message. As soon as I see how things are going to fall out for me here, I plan to send him off. And then I'm hoping and praying to be right on his heels.

But for right now, I'm dispatching Epaphroditus, my good friend and companion in my work. You sent him to help me out; now I'm sending him to help you out. He has been wanting in the worst way to get back with you. Especially since recovering from the illness you heard about, he's been wanting to get back and reassure you that he is just fine. He nearly died, as you know, but God had mercy on him. And not only on him—he had mercy on me, too. His death would have been one huge grief piled on top of all the others.

So you can see why I'm so delighted to send him on to you. When you see him again, hale and hearty, how you'll rejoice and how relieved I'll be. Give him a grand welcome, a joyful embrace! People like him deserve the best you can give. Remember the ministry to me that you started but weren't able to complete? Well, in the process of finishing up that work, he put his life on the line and nearly died doing it.

THINK

"I took all this in and thought it through, inside and out." (Ecclesiastes 9:1)

• What thoughts or feelings do these words evoke in you? Try to pinpoint why.

- About Epaphroditus, Paul writes, "Give him a grand welcome, a joyful embrace!" Can you remember a time when you felt welcomed somewhere in such a way? Describe your feelings then. What can you imitate from that time so others always feel welcomed by you?
- If you were to send a couple of friends to help a young church, who would you send and why?

READ

From *31 Days of Praise* by Ruth and Warren Myers[1]

Day 19

Thank You, Lord, for the people who are a blessing to me . . . for family and friends and neighbors, for little children, for brothers and sisters in Christ, for colleagues and leaders, for pastors and teachers . . . and for others: our doctor, the postman, the plumber. Thank you for the many ways You use these people to meet my needs, brighten my path, and lighten my load . . . to enrich my knowledge of You, and to counsel or correct or nourish me, building me up in the faith. How good and how pleasant it is to enjoy rich fellowship with those who love You. Thank You for bringing people into my life!

THINK

"I took all this in and thought it through, inside and out." (Ecclesiastes 9:1)

- Look back at Myers' words and notice who she lists as a blessing to her. Take some time to thank God for the people who fill these roles in your own life. Maybe write down their names so you can pray for them regularly.
- Don't just rush through your list of names. Beside each name, jot a few notes about how God uses that person to meet needs, brighten your path, lighten your load, and so on.

READ

From *Twelve Baskets of Crumbs* by Elisabeth Elliot[2]

'M' is for a Merry Heart

Special occasions like Mother's Day put different kinds of burdens on different people. Those whose work involves expressing themselves publicly usually feel that on such occasions they "ought to say something" appropriate to the day. At first I shied away from this, because I always shy away from things that might turn out to be soupy. But as I thought more about it I realized that it wasn't a question of "ought to" but a good excuse to write down just one or two things, at least, about a remarkable mother I know very well—my own. And if I write about her it won't be soupy.

She is nearly 72 years old now, and that fact, coupled with people's applying to her adjectives like "alert" and "spry" and "very much alive," reminds me that she is in the category of "old." People certainly don't use those adjectives much for other age groups. But it is hard to think of Katherine Gillingham Howard as old.

THINK "I took all this in and thought it through, inside and out." (Ecclesiastes 9:1)

- Take a few moments and think about your parents. They might be alive or dead. Whatever situation existed as you were growing up, whether your parents were remarkable or harsh and destructive, try to write down at least one or two things about your parents. Don't make it soupy; make it honest.
- Look at what you've written about your parents. Whether it's mostly positive or mostly negative, can you find at least one thing to praise or thank God for? It might even be something you learned in the midst of a bad situation.

THINK (continued)

READ

From *Winter: Notes from Montana* by Rick Bass[3]

September 20

(Bass lives in the Yaak valley in northwest Montana. This account from his journal recounts aspects of his first winter there; Bass realized he knew little about anything.)

It can be so wonderful, finding out you were wrong, that you are ignorant, that you know nothing, not squat. You get to start over. It's like snow, falling that first time each year. It doesn't make any sound, but it's the strongest force you know of. Trees will crack and pop and split open later in the winter. Things opening up, learning. Learning the way it really is.

THINK

"I took all this in and thought it through, inside and out." (Ecclesiastes 9:1)

- Have you ever had a similar experience where you joyfully realized how ignorant you are? If so, talk about it with your group. If not, how do you think this kind of experience would affect you?
- How old do you think most people are when they realize that they "know nothing, not squat"? What do you base your answer on?
- Where do you think you are when it comes to "learning the way it really is"? Explain.

READ

From *Resistance* by Barry Lopez[4]

Apocalypse

We reject the assertion, promoted today by success-mongering bull terriers in business, in government, in religion, that humans are goal-seeking animals. We believe they are creatures in search of proportion in life, a pattern of grace. It is balance and beauty we believe people want, not triumph. The stories the earth's peoples adhere to with greatest faith—the dances that topple fearful walls; the ethereal performances of light, color, and music; the enduring musics themselves—are all well patterned . . . these patterns from the artesian wells of artistic impulse do not require updating. They only require repetition.

THINK   "I took all this in and thought it through, inside and out." (Ecclesiastes 9:1)

- What about you—do you accept or reject the assertion that "humans are goal-seeking animals"? Why?
- "The dances that topple fearful walls"—sounds like a good description of joy, doesn't it? What other action words (such as "dance") would you use to describe your own experiences of joy?

PRAY

Slowly read the following poem a couple of times. What speaks to you? Ask God to bring a word or phrase to the surface. Then allow that word or phrase to begin your prayer. It might seem awkward at first. Fine, let it be awkward. But stick with it.

The Faces I Love

In the end I will have my own chair.
I will pull the blinds down and watch my nose and mouth
in the blistered glass.
I will look back in amazement at what I did
and cry aloud for two more years, for four more years,
just to remember the faces, just to recall the names,
to put them back together—
the names I can't forget, the faces I love.

— GERALD STERN[5]

LIVE

These words from Stern serve as a reminder of this section's theme—*joy*:

>I will look back in amazement . . .
>just to remember the faces, just to recall the names.

You've read from the journal entries, letters, and poems of others. Now it's your turn. What does God want you to live when it comes to *joy*? Use the space below to write a letter to yourself. You might want to date the letter so you can reflect later where you were and what was going on in your life regarding *joy*.

Date _____

Dear _____

APPEARANCES

"Steer clear of the barking dogs, those religious busybodies, all bark and no bite. All they're interested in is appearances."

(PHILIPPIANS 3:2)

Before You Begin

Take just a few moments to still your heart and mind. Remember, God desires to speak to *you* in these moments.

> *Over and over God rescued them,*
> *but they never learned—*
> *until finally their sins destroyed them.*

PSALM 106:43

READ

Philippians 3:1-6

And that's about it, friends. Be glad in God!

I don't mind repeating what I have written in earlier letters, and I hope you don't mind hearing it again. Better safe than sorry—so here goes.

Steer clear of the barking dogs, those religious busybodies, all bark and no bite. All they're interested in is appearances— knife-happy circumcisers, I call them. The *real* believers are the ones the Spirit of God leads to work away at this ministry, filling the air with Christ's praise as we do it. We couldn't carry this off by our own efforts, and we know it—even though we can list what many might think are impressive credentials. You know my pedigree: a legitimate birth, circumcised on the eighth day; an Israelite from the elite tribe of Benjamin; a strict and devout adherent to God's law; a fiery defender of the purity of my religion, even to the point of persecuting the church; a meticulous observer of everything set down in God's law Book.

THINK

"I took all this in and thought it through, inside and out." (Ecclesiastes 9:1)

- Paul writes that he's addressed the topic of religious busybodies in earlier letters. Apparently they were a significant problem in the early church! What other words or images stir in you when you hear that phrase, "religious busybodies"?
- Paul continues by saying that all these people are only interested in appearances. Do you think the same can be said about some people in churches today? Explain.

THINK (continued)

READ

From *The Relentless Tenderness of Jesus* by Brennan Manning[1]

Freedom Under the Word

(Manning has just described the difference between
Pioneer and Settler Theology. The breakdown is as follows:

PIONEER	SETTLER
church=covered wagon	church=courthouse
God=trail boss	God=mayor
Jesus=scout	Jesus=sheriff
Holy Spirit=buffalo hunter	Holy Spirit=saloon girl
clergyman=cook	clergyman=banker
faith=spirit of adventure	faith=trusting in the safety of the town
sin=wanting to turn back	sin=breaking a town ordinance)

The settlers and the pioneers portray in cowboy-movie language the people of the law and the people of the Spirit. In the time of the historical Jesus, the guardians of the ecclesiastical setup, the scribes and Pharisees and Sadducees, had ensconced themselves in the courthouse and enslaved themselves to the law. This not only enhanced their prestige in society, it also gave them a sense of security. People fear the responsibility of being free. It is easier to let others make the decisions or to rely upon the letter of the law. Some people want to be slaves.

After enslaving themselves to the letter of the law, such people always go on to deny freedom to others. They will not rest until they have imposed the same oppressive burdens upon others.

THINK "I took all this in and thought it through, inside and out." (Ecclesiastes 9:1)

- Would you rather be a pioneer or a settler? Why?
- Which are you in reality? If you asked two or three close friends to place one of these labels on you, which would they choose?

- This will take some time, but can you think of contemporary equivalents for pioneers and settlers? Maybe your groups come from different generations or from different denominations. How does each one see church, God, Jesus, the Spirit, and the other terms on Manning's list?

READ

From *The Memory of Old Jack* by Wendell Berry[2]

Through the Valley

(Jack Beechum, a farmer, is a man of the land and its rhythms. Clara,
Jack's daughter, married Gladston Pettit and moved to the city. This
scene follows the death of Jack's wife, Ruth, when he makes an offer to
his son-in-law.)

And so one Sunday afternoon Jack took Glad over there and
showed him the farm and told him what he had on his mind,
or most of it. Glad was no longer the lean and muscular man he
had been when he married. He was fleshy now and somewhat
stooped in the shoulders; he had been more weakened by the
last fifteen years than Jack had been by the last fifty. But his
superfluous weight, covered as it was by a tailored suit, set off by
his graying hair, a diamond ring, and an excellent cigar, somehow
made him look richer, more substantial, more implicitly dignified
than ever. As his consort, Clara had become plump and opulent.
Though she was still pretty, her looks had somehow become
merely decorative. She had made of herself a sort of portable
occasion for the ostentatious gifts of her husband, a sort of bodi-
less apparition in fine clothes—useless, so far as Jack could tell,
for either work or love.

"There it is," Jack told him. "You can have it, I think, at a
good price. And you can take care of it and make it a satisfaction
to you. And it'll be there when you need it."

Even as he spoke he realized how little pleased he was by the
vision he was conjuring up. He disliked the idea of a man *retir-
ing* to a farm. He disliked the idea of a man living on land that he
thought himself too good to dirty his hands in. So far as he was
concerned, a man who thought he was better than such dirt as
he and Glad had underneath their feet that Sunday was a good
deal worse.

As Jack should have known, Glad did not buy the farm. . . .

What he had done, Jack realized, was make a good plan
and then invent a man to go with it. What he had imagined

had certainly had no relation to any possibility that was in Glad Pettit. And though he was more than a little relieved that the farm had not been bought by a man so unworthy of it, the incident confirmed his until now unacknowledged contempt for Glad Pettit and all that he stood for. . . . As had come to be his way, he just flatly accepted that his daughter and son-in-law were of a kind that was estranged and alien, and probably inimical, to his kind. A man without a place that he respects, he thought, may do *anything* with money.

THINK   "I took all this in and thought it through, inside and out." (Ecclesiastes 9:1)

- Do you know people like Gladston and Clara? Do you know anyone like Jack? How are the people you know similar and different from the ones in this reading?
- This Letter is about appearances. What stood out as Berry described each character?
- Like Jack in this story, have you found yourself making either good or bad assumptions about the people you know based on their appearances or credentials? How do you think that meshes with what Paul writes in Philippians 3:1-6?

READ

From *The Lives of Rocks* by Rick Bass[3]

The Lives of Rocks

(Jyl is a cancer survivor, living alone in a mountain cabin.
Her closest neighbors are the Workmans.)

Her nearest neighbors were a fundamentalist Christian family named Workman, a name that had always made her laugh, for she had rarely seen them *not* working: the mother, the father, and the five children—three boys and two girls, ranging in age from fourteen to two.

The Workmans lived only a few miles away as a raven flew, though it was many miles by rutted road to drive to the head of their valley—and even then a long walk in was required. They lived without electricity or running water or indoor plumbing or refrigeration or telephone, and they often were without a car that ran. They owned five acres downstream along the creek, the same creek that Jyl lived by, in the next valley over, and they had a fluctuating menagerie of chickens, milk cows, pigs, goats, horses, ponies, and turkeys.

When they traveled to town, which was not often, difficult as it was for them to get out of their valley, they were as likely to ride single file on a procession of odd-sized and strangely colored, strangely shaped horses and ponies as they were to travel in one of their decrepit vehicles, smoke rings rising from both the front and back ends as it chugged down the ragged road.

No family ever worked harder, and it seemed to Jyl sometimes that their God was a god of labor rather than mercy or forgiveness.

THINK   "I took all this in and thought it through, inside and out." (Ecclesiastes 9:1)

- Do you know anyone like the Workmans? How are the people you know similar and different from them?

- Are you like the Workmans in any way?
- Again, this Letter is about appearances. What stood out as you read Bass's description of this family and the way they lived?
- "Their God was a god of labor rather than mercy or forgiveness." Take some time to reflect on that quote. Where does your mind take you?

READ

From *The Divine Embrace* by Ken Gire[4]

Transformed by a Face

Thomas Dubay, in his book *The Evidential Power of Beauty*, tells a story about a teenage girl in the atheistic Soviet Union who knew nothing of the Bible, nothing of the doctrines of the church, nothing of the differences between denominations. She also knew nothing of Jesus. Until one day she chanced upon a copy of Luke's gospel. When she finished reading it, her immediate reaction was, "I fell in love with him."

Isn't that beautiful?

"I fell in love with him." . . .

We are not transformed by a curriculum; we are transformed by a person. And we are transformed not by studying that person but by beholding him. Busyness is not conducive to beholding. . . .

A lot of busyness stems from individual and corporate efforts aimed at helping people get over their struggles so they can go on to maturity. In *The Pursuit of God*, A.W. Tozer describes what I believe is a better model: "The man who has struggled to purify himself and has had nothing but repeated failures will experience real relief when he stops tinkering with his soul and looks away to the perfect One. While he looks at Christ, the very things he has so long been trying to do will be getting done within him. It will be God working in him to will and to do."

Love changes us in ways that law cannot. Spiritual formation, a term used to describe the process of being changed into the image of Christ, doesn't happen by following disciplines. It happens by falling in love. When we fall in love with Jesus, all the other loves in our life fall into place. And those that once competed with Christ now subordinate themselves to him. Everything in our life finds its proper value once we have properly valued him.

THINK   *"I took all this in and thought it through, inside and out."* (Ecclesiastes 9:1)

- Would you say your life is one of busyness or one of beholding? Explain how you got to this point.
- Ponder the following statement: "When we fall in love with Jesus, all the other loves in our life fall into place." Do you think this is true? Does it describe something that has happened to you? Does it describe how you feel about Jesus now, or have you lost this feeling? If not, how do you relate to Jesus?

PRAY

Slowly read the following song a couple of times. What speaks to you?
Ask God to bring a word or phrase to the surface. Then allow that
word or phrase to begin your prayer. It might seem awkward at first.
Fine, let it be awkward. But stick with it.

Near to the Heart of God

There is a place of quiet rest,
Near to the heart of God.
A place where sin cannot molest,
Near to the heart of God.
O Jesus, blest Redeemer,
Sent from the heart of God,
Hold us who wait before Thee
Near to the heart of God.

—CLELAND B. McAFEE[5]

LIVE

These words from McAfee serve as a reminder of this section's
theme—*appearances*:

> Hold us who wait before Thee
> Near to the heart of God.

You've read from the journal entries, letters, and poems of
others. Now it's your turn. What does God want you to live when it
comes to *appearances*? Use the space below to write a letter to yourself. You might want to date the letter so you can reflect later where
you were and what was going on in your life regarding *appearances*.

Date _____

Dear _____

"I gave up all that inferior stuff so I could
know Christ personally."
(PHILIPPIANS 3:10)

Before You Begin

Take just a few moments to still your heart and mind.
Remember, God desires to speak to *you* in these
moments.

> *GOD, my God,*
> *I can't thank you enough.*
>
> PSALM 30:12

READ

Philippians 3:7-11

The very credentials these people are waving around as something special, I'm tearing up and throwing out with the trash—along with everything else I used to take credit for. And why? Because of Christ. Yes, all the things I once thought were so important are gone from my life. Compared to the high privilege of knowing Christ Jesus as my Master, firsthand, everything I once thought I had going for me is insignificant—dog dung. I've dumped it all in the trash so that I could embrace Christ and be embraced by him. I didn't want some petty, inferior brand of righteousness that comes from keeping a list of rules when I could get the robust kind that comes from trusting Christ—*God's* righteousness.

I gave up all that inferior stuff so I could know Christ personally, experience his resurrection power, be a partner in his suffering, and go all the way with him to death itself. If there was any way to get in on the resurrection from the dead, I wanted to do it.

THINK

"I took all this in and thought it through, inside and out." (Ecclesiastes 9:1)

- What are some things—you can be as general or as specific as you want—that you once considered important but not anymore? What changed?
- What about spiritually? What areas used to be hills to die on but now are not? What changed?
- Do you find yourself scoring your spiritual life on a list of rules? Score it from 1 (all rules) to 10 (no rules). Share your score with the group and explain it.

THINK (continued)

READ

From *Between Noon and Three* by Robert Farrar Capon[1]

Sticks, Stones, and Snake Oil

While we were yet sinners, Christ died for the ungodly. It is he that reconciles me, not the law; for by its very truth, the law shows me only that I am unreconciled. My many transgressions in the past, permitted or not—and my many transgressions in the future, including, perhaps, the founding of a cult that feeds babies to crocodiles—stand against me. But the gospel of grace says that God does not stand against me, that he is not and never will be my enemy, and that he has so arranged things by the mystery of Christ's death and resurrection that at any time—before, during, or after any of my sins, past or future—I can come to him just for the coming and find myself at home.

Do you see that what that says is far more shocking than the worst shock I may have given you—that it means that I may well be wicked at any time, but that I am free for all time of any condemnation for my wickedness? And that therefore I am free to be wicked, monumentally or shakily, alone or with others, in thought, word, or deed—and with no limits upper or lower my whole life long—*and still remain free of my wickedness?* Was there any way I could have told you that truth without some shock to your system? Indeed, I begin only just now to see some validity to your point about insufficient outrageousness. Your failure to grasp the point of grace leads me to think you may have been right. It is not exactly that I trifled with you; but perhaps I did over-entertain you. I served you a delicate little fillet of dalliance when I should have rammed a whole, uncooked fish down your throat.

One footnote. If we are ever to enter fully into the glorious liberty of the children of God, we are going to have to spend more time thinking about freedom than we do. The church, by and large, has had a poor record of encouraging freedom. It has spent so much time inculcating in us the fear of making mistakes that it has made us like ill-taught piano students: we play our pieces, but we never really hear them because our main concern is not to make music, but to avoid some flub that will get us in Dutch. The church . . . has been so afraid we will lose sight of the laws of our nature that it has made us care more about how we look than about who we are—made us act more like the subjects of a police state than fellow citizens of the saints.

THINK   *"I took all this in and thought it through, inside and out." (Ecclesiastes 9:1)*

- You might have to read this more than once, because Capon lays it on pretty heavily. What seemed to speak to you as you read this passage? What "shocked" you?
- Respond to this statement: "The church, by and large, has had a poor record of encouraging freedom." Is that true in your experience? What do you think the church—the one composed of all Christians or your own congregation—would look like if it encouraged freedom?

READ

From *Abba's Child* by Brennan Manning[2]

Present Risenness

The resurrection of Jesus must be experienced as more than a past historical event. Otherwise, "it is robbed of its impact on the present." In his book *True Resurrection*, Anglican theologian H. A. Williams wrote, "That is why for most of the time resurrection means little to us. It is remote and isolated. And that is why for the majority of people it means nothing. . . . People do well to be skeptical of beliefs not anchored in present experience."

On the other hand, if the central saving act of Christian faith is relegated to the future with the fervent hope that Christ's resurrection is the pledge of our own and that one day we shall reign with Him in glory, then the risen One is pushed safely out of the present. Limiting the resurrection either to the past or to the future makes the present risenness of Jesus largely irrelevant, safeguards us from interference with the ordinary rounds and daily routine of our lives, and preempts communion *now* with Jesus as a living person.

THINK   "I took all this in and thought it through, inside and out." (Ecclesiastes 9:1)

- Where is Jesus' resurrection for you? In the past? Future? A present reality?
- Would you say that Christ is active in your life right now? How? Be as specific as you can about how Jesus affects "the ordinary rounds and daily routine" of your life.
- Do you think of Jesus as "a living person"? If so, what makes him real to you? If not, describe how you do think of Jesus.

THINK (continued)

READ

From *Dangerous Wonder* by Michael Yaconelli[3]

The Obstacle of Dullness

What happened to radical Christianity, the un-nice brand of Christianity that turned the world upside-down? What happened to the category-smashing, life-threatening, anti-institutional gospel that spread through the first century like wildfire and was considered (by those in power) dangerous? What happened to the kind of Christians whose hearts were on fire, who had no fear, who spoke the truth no matter what the consequence, who made the world uncomfortable, who were willing to follow Jesus wherever He went? What happened to the kind of Christians who were filled with passion and gratitude, and who every day were unable to get over the grace of God? . . .

The Bible names our problem: *sin*. Don't let the word fool you. Sin is more than turning our backs on God; it is turning our backs on *life*! Immorality is much more than adultery and dishonesty, it is *living drab, colorless, dreary, stale, unimaginative lives*. The greatest enemy of Christianity may be people who say they believe in Jesus but who are no longer astonished and amazed. Jesus Christ came to rescue us from listlessness as well as lostness; He came to save us from flat souls as well as corrupted souls. He came to save us from dullness. Our culture is awash in immorality and drowning in dullness. We have forgotten how to dance, how to sing, and how to laugh. . . . We have been stunted by mediocrity.

THINK   "I took all this in and thought it through, inside and out." (Ecclesiastes 9:1)

- If you had to explain *grace* to an elementary Sunday school student, what brief definition would you use? How does this excerpt connect with your concept of grace?
- In Philippians 3:9, Paul writes about "the robust kind [of

righteousness] that comes from trusting Christ." Do you think that's what Yaconelli refers to? Or is it something else? Explain.

- "We have forgotten how to dance, how to sing, and how to laugh," Yaconelli writes. Recall the last time you did any one of those three things. How did your action connect to your relationship with God? When it comes to your faith, what makes you afraid to dance, sing, and laugh? Do you want to change that?

READ

From *Orthodoxy* by G. K. Chesterton[4]

The Eternal Revolution

It is one of the hundred answers to the fugitive perversion of modern "force" that the promptest and boldest agencies are also the most fragile or full of sensibility. The swiftest things are the softest things. A bird is active, because a bird is soft. A stone is helpless, because a stone is hard. The stone must by its own nature go downwards, because hardness is weakness. The bird can of its nature go upwards, because fragility is force. In perfect force there is a kind of frivolity, an airiness that can maintain itself in the air. Modern investigators of miraculous history have solemnly admitted that a characteristic of the great saints is their power of "levitation." They might go further; a characteristic of the great saints is their power of levity. Angels can fly because they take themselves lightly.

THINK "I took all this in and thought it through, inside and out." (Ecclesiastes 9:1)

• Based on Chesterton's words, if your friends had to choose between *bird* or *rock* to describe you, which would they pick?

• How would you describe yourself? Another way of answering is to think about whether you consider yourself a serious or lighthearted person. Do you like that or wish it were different?

• When was the last time you lightened up on yourself? If it was a long time ago, think about why you're so hard on yourself.

THINK (continued)

PRAY

Slowly read the following poem a couple of times. What speaks to
you? Ask God to bring a word or phrase to the surface. Then allow
that word or phrase to begin your prayer. It might seem awkward at
first. Fine, let it be awkward. But stick with it.

> For I tell you this; one loving blind desire for God alone
> is more valuable in itself, more pleasing to God and to
> the saints, more beneficial to your own growth, and more
> helpful to your friends, both living and dead, than
> anything else you could do.[5]

LIVE

These words serve as a reminder of this section's theme—*grace*:

One loving blind desire for God alone.

You've read from the journal entries, letters, and poems of others. Now it's your turn. What does God want you to live when it comes to *grace*? Use the space below to write a letter to yourself. You might want to date the letter so you can reflect later where you were and what was going on in your life regarding *grace*.

Date _____

Dear _____

FOCUS

"God will clear your blurred vision—you'll see it yet!
Now that we're on the right track, let's stay on it."
(Philippians 3:15-16)

Before You Begin

Take just a few moments to still your heart and mind.
Remember, God desires to speak to *you* in these
moments.

> God-of-the-Angel-Armies, come back!
> *Smile your blessing smile:*
> That *will be our salvation.*
>
> PSALM 80:7

READ

Philippians 3:15-21

So let's keep focused on that goal, those of us who want everything God has for us. If any of you have something else in mind, something less than total commitment, God will clear your blurred vision—you'll see it yet! Now that we're on the right track, let's stay on it.

Stick with me, friends. Keep track of those you see running this same course, headed for this same goal. There are many out there taking other paths, choosing other goals, and trying to get you to go along with them. I've warned you of them many times; sadly, I'm having to do it again. All they want is easy street. They hate Christ's Cross. But easy street is a dead-end street. Those who live there make their bellies their gods; belches are their praise; all they can think of is their appetites.

But there's far more to life for us. We're citizens of high heaven! We're waiting the arrival of the Savior, the Master, Jesus Christ, who will transform our earthy bodies into glorious bodies like his own. He'll make us beautiful and whole with the same powerful skill by which he is putting everything as it should be, under and around him.

THINK   "I took all this in and thought it through, inside and out." (Ecclesiastes 9:1)

- In what ways do you see some people wanting to live spiritually on "easy street"?
- Would you describe that way of living as hating "Christ's Cross," or do you think Paul is exaggerating?
- Paul writes that "those of us who want everything God has for us" experience "far more to life." Does this describe you? Do you wish it did? Explain.

THINK (continued)

READ

From *Walking on Water* by Madeleine L'Engle[1]

Healed, Whole and Holy

We are still being taught that fairy tales and myths are to be discarded as soon as we are old enough to understand "reality." I had a disturbed and angry letter from a young mother who told me that a friend of hers, with young children, gave them only instructive books; she wasn't going to allow their minds to be polluted with fairy tales. They were going to be taught the "real" world.

This attitude is a victory for the powers of this world. A friend of mine, a fine story-teller, remarked to me, "Jesus was not a theologian. He was God who told stories."

Yes. God who told stories.

St. Matthew says, "And he spake many things to them in parables . . . and without a parable spake he not to them."

When the powers of this world denigrate and deny the value of story, life loses much of its meaning; and for many people in the world today, life *has* lost its meaning, one reason why every other hospital bed is for someone with a mental, not a physical illness.

THINK   "I took all this in and thought it through, inside and out." (Ecclesiastes 9:1)

- What's your favorite Bible story? Why?
- How has that story helped you glimpse the meaning of your own life? Do you think it has helped you step closer to the goal of becoming more like Christ?
- The verse L'Engle quotes reads like this in *The Message*: "All Jesus did that day was tell stories—a long storytelling afternoon" (Matthew 13:34). What would it be like to spend a day or an afternoon listening to Jesus tell stories?

THINK (continued)

READ

From *Waking the Dead* by John Eldredge[2]

Mythic Reality

Former Wheaton College president Clyde Kilby explains, "Myth is the name of a way of seeing, a way of *knowing*." Not fantasy, not lies, but things coming to us from beyond the walls of this world. Rolland Hein observes, "They are the kind of story that wakes you up, and suddenly you say, 'Yes, yes, this is what my life has really been about! Here is where my meaning and my destiny lie!'" And we need some waking up, you and I. We are, for the most part, alert and oriented times zero.

Years ago a mother wrote to C. S. Lewis regarding her son (age nine) and his love for *The Chronicles of Narnia*. The boy was feeling bad because he felt he loved Aslan (the lion hero of the story) more than Jesus. With grace and brilliance Lewis replied that he need not worry: "For the things he loves Aslan for doing or saying are simply the things that Jesus really did and said. So that when Laurence thinks he is loving Aslan, he is really loving Jesus: and perhaps loving Him more than he ever did before." Truth doesn't need a verse attached to it to be true. All that you loved about Aslan *is* Jesus. . . .

Mythic stories help us to see clearly, which is to say, they help us see with the eyes of the heart.

THINK *"I took all this in and thought it through, inside and out."* (Ecclesiastes 9:1)

- Reread Philippians 3:15-21 at the beginning of this Letter. How do you think Eldredge's words connect with Paul's words? There's not necessarily a right or easy answer—you might need to wrestle with this awhile.
- Can you think of a character in a novel or a movie who you just loved—if you're completely honest, perhaps who you

loved more than Jesus? What about that character captured your heart?

- Did this character help you realize something about your life? In other words, how did that character or the story help you round out your life by illustrating something true, whether it was true of you, the world, or Jesus?

READ

From *Ragman and Other Cries of Faith* by Walter Wangerin Jr.[3]

Preaching

Or what, for heaven's sake, is the incarnation, if it doesn't announce God's personal immersion in the events—the bloody events, the insignificant and humbly common events, the physical and social and painful and peaceful and daily and epochal events of the lives of the people? In their experience! And isn't the coming of the Holy Spirit the setting free of that immersion, so that it be not restricted to any sole place, time, or people, but breathes through *all* experience and temples in *every* faithful breast?

Of course. Of course. It is hard not to argue the immanence of God. Why, it is one of our doctrines.

One of our doctrines. There's the sticking point. So long as it remains a doctrine alone, a truth to be taught, immanence itself continues an abstraction—and is not immanent. God abides not only in the church, but in the books of the church, and in the minds that explain the books, and in the intellect.

What then, Priests? Preachers, what shall we do that the people's perception of God not be so much less than God himself?

Make something more of our preaching. Allow the preaching itself a human—and then a divine—*wholeness*: that the whole of the preacher be presently active in proclamation, the whole of the hearer invited to attend, and God will be seen as God of the Whole.

Or, to rush the point: tell stories.

THINK   "I took all this in and thought it through, inside and out." (Ecclesiastes 9:1)

- Respond to this statement: "God abides not only in the church, but in the books of the church, and in the minds that explain the books, and in the intellect."

- In Philippians 3:15-21, Paul cautions against taking "easy
  street." Based on Wangerin's words, how might the doctrine/
  classroom approach be taking the easy way spiritually? You
  might have to dig deep on this one.

READ

From *The Language of Life* by Bill Moyers[4]

Joy Harjo

(Moyers is interviewing the poet, Joy Harjo. She was born to a Creek
father and a French-Cherokee mother and claims that her voice is often
guided by an old Creek Indian within her. She teaches at the University
of Arizona in Tucson.)

Moyers: Tell me about your family.

Harjo: I suppose the person who influenced me the most was
my Aunt Lois Harjo Ball. She was a painter, and I was always
amazed by what she could remember. In fact, I've always been
amazed at what native people can remember. Native people are
generally from oral cultures—they may be able to read and write,
sometimes even in their own language, but the expression of the
culture is primarily oral. So they're incredibly gifted in memory
and in telling stories. . . .

Moyers: Did these stories come down through the generations
as a kind of poetry?

Harjo: Yes, they *are* a kind of poetry, and I greatly admire the
speakers, those who keep the stories alive. My paternal grand-
father was a Creek Baptist minister, and although he died long
before I was born, I always recognize something of his life in
what I am doing. I love the ability to tell a story and to tell it well.
Traditionally, wealth was often determined by your gifts in this
area. How many songs do you know? How many stories can you
tell? And how *well* can you tell them? I think the skills which
enabled the retelling of memory were seen as our *true* riches.

THINK   "I took all this in and thought it through, inside and
out." (Ecclesiastes 9:1)

* In your family, do you remember someone who served as
  the storyteller? If that person isn't around anymore, has
  someone taken his or her place? Or has that become a place
  of poverty in your life?

• Many of the readings in this Letter have been about the life-enriching power of stories. How do stories help clear your vision so you can focus on the goal?

PRAY

Slowly read the following poem a couple of times. What speaks to you? Ask God to bring a word or phrase to the surface. Then allow that word or phrase to begin your prayer. It might seem awkward at first. Fine, let it be awkward. But stick with it.

I Ask My Mother to Sing

She begins, and my grandmother joins her.
Mother and daughter sing like young girls.
If my father were alive, he would play
his accordion and sway like a boat.
I've never been in Peking, or the Summer Palace,
nor stood on the great Stone Boat to watch
the rain begin on Kuen Ming Lake, the picnickers
running away from the grass.
But I love to hear it sung:
how the waterlilies fill with rain until
they overturn, spilling water into water,
then rock back, and fill with more.
Both women have begun to cry.
But neither stops her song.

— LI-YOUNG LEE[5]

LIVE

These words from Lee serve as a reminder of this section's theme —*focus*:

> But I love to hear it sung.

You've read from the journal entries, letters, and poems of others. Now it's your turn. What does God want you to live when it comes to *focus*? Use the space below to write a letter to yourself. You might want to date the letter so you can reflect later where you were and what was going on in your life regarding *focus*.

Date _____

Dear _____

CELEBRATION

"Celebrate God all day, every day. I mean, *revel* in him!"
(PHILIPPIANS 4:4)

Before You Begin

Take just a few moments to still your heart and mind. Remember, God desires to speak to *you* in these moments.

So thank GOD for his marvelous love,
for his miracle mercy to the children he loves.

PSALM 107:8

READ

Philippians 4:4-9

Celebrate God all day, every day. I mean, *revel* in him! Make it as clear as you can to all you meet that you're on their side, working with them and not against them. Help them see that the Master is about to arrive. He could show up any minute!

Don't fret or worry. Instead of worrying, pray. Let petitions and praises shape your worries into prayers, letting God know your concerns. Before you know it, a sense of God's wholeness, everything coming together for good, will come and settle you down. It's wonderful what happens when Christ displaces worry at the center of your life.

Summing it all up, friends, I'd say you'll do best by filling your minds and meditating on things true, noble, reputable, authentic, compelling, gracious—the best, not the worst; the beautiful, not the ugly; things to praise, not things to curse. Put into practice what you learned from me, what you heard and saw and realized. Do that, and God, who makes everything work together, will work you into his most excellent harmonies.

THINK

"I took all this in and thought it through, inside and out." (Ecclesiastes 9:1)

- Paul writes, "Help them see that the Master . . . could show up any minute!" Do you think you can show the people around you that Christ is about to arrive simply by celebrating? How would that look in your life? Be specific.
- "Instead of worrying, pray." Paul's words sound so incredibly simple. Do you think he's being realistic? Why or why not?
- If you filled your mind, today, with "things noble . . . compelling . . . beautiful" and so on, what would those "things" be? Let this answer gel in your mind awhile.

THINK (continued)

READ

From *The Book of Yaak* by Rick Bass[1]

The Fringe

(Bass lives in the remote Yaak valley in northwestern Montana. The inhabitants are few and far between.)

Way upvalley there is an old woman who swims in the frigid Yaak River. I use the phrase "old woman" with nothing but the utmost respect. . . .

Her name is Jeannette Nolan McIntire. She and her husband, John, were artists right from the very beginning. She was born in San Francisco, and studied acting and opera; he was born in Hog Heaven, Montana—the next valley over—and studied, well, loving the woods. . . .

Mrs. McIntire tells a story of how there was art buried even beneath the foundation of one of the old outbuildings on their property, when they first moved up here. There was a trapper's cabin next to their barn, built right after the turn of the century, and it had a little earthen basement. The trapper had used this basement for storage—a desk, a chair, and some wooden crates—and over the years, some of the dirt walls had crumbled in over these things. One day the McIntires were down there, *excavating*, and they opened those wooden crates and found that while the trapper had been living up there by himself through those long winters, he had been writing plays—reams and reams of plays.

"And they were beautiful," Mrs. McIntire says. "We sat there and read those plays, and thought about him living here so long ago, just writing these beautiful plays, and we just cried."

THINK

"I took all this in and thought it through, inside and out." (Ecclesiastes 9:1)

• Choose a word or two to describe how this passage makes you feel. Don't focus on *think*, but on *feel*.

- For the McIntires to fill their minds, they had to work a little. It took some "excavating," or looking. How would you rate your excavation skills? Do you experience beauty every day, or do you struggle to keep "noble" as part of your vocabulary?

READ

From *Fire in the Belly* by Sam Keen[2]

A Primer for Now and Future Heroes

Ten years ago, after remarriage and beginning a second family, I
built a small cabin near the house. First I placed in it all the practical things I needed to be comfortable and nurture myself—a
wood stove, a small kitchen, a toilet, a bed, a table, an outdoor
shower. Next I turned the cabin into a personal sanctuary by
bringing into it all the icons and sacred objects I had collected
from childhood—objects that carry a part of my story. Cherished
pieces of driftwood, rocks picked up at memorable times, Indian
rugs my father gave me before he died, a picture painted for
me by a friend, a cobalt blue bottle, my desert-island books, etc.
Once my cabin was finished I began my practice. . . . One or two
nights a week I prepared my own dinner, ate alone by candle-
light, smoked my pipe in front of the fire, sat in the rocker, considered my days, slept by myself, caught my dreams.

THINK   "I took all this in and thought it through, inside and
out." (Ecclesiastes 9:1)

- You might not have the resources to build a cabin near your
  house as Keen did, but can you think of a space in your
  home or apartment or room to make a personal sanctuary?
  If you placed objects in that space representing truth, nobil-
  ity, authenticity, graciousness, and beauty, what would you
  choose? Make a list and mentally place them in your space.
- Do you think a space like this would help you fill your mind
  with the good and true and beautiful? Why or why not?

THINK (continued)

READ

From *A River Runs Through It* by Norman Maclean[3]

Learning to Read

I sat there and forgot and forgot, until what remained was the river that went by and I who watched. . . . Eventually the watcher joined the river, and there was only one of us. I believe it was the river. . . .

As the heat mirages on the river in front of me danced with and through each other, I could feel patterns from my own life joining with them. It was here, while waiting for my brother, that I started this story, although, of course, at the time I did not know that stories of life are more often like rivers than books. But I knew a story had begun, perhaps long ago near the sound of water. And I sensed that ahead I would meet something that would never erode so there would be a sharp turn, deep circles, a deposit and quietness.

The fisherman even has a phrase to describe what he does when he studies the patterns of a river. He says he is "reading the water," and perhaps to tell his stories he has to do much the same thing. Then one of his biggest problems is to guess where and at what time of day life lies ready to be taken as a joke. And to guess whether it is going to be a little or a big joke. For all of us, though, it is much easier to read the waters of tragedy.

THINK "I took all this in and thought it through, inside and out." (Ecclesiastes 9:1)

- Maclean fills his mind with the beautiful and noble using nature and memory. Name a place you cherished as a child, a place you *knew*. What memories surface when you ponder that place? Are they happy, sad, or somewhere in between?
- Have you learned to read your life? Do you look back through the waters of memory and tell the stories of where

you came from and who you are and what your belief in God looks like and how much you love your children or whatever? Whether they involve laughter or tragedy, the stories need to be told.

READ

From *Peace Like a River* by Lief Enger[4]

Clay

When I was born to Helen and Jeremiah Land, in 1951, my lungs refused to kick in. . . .

Dad had gone out to pace in the damp September wind. He was praying, rounding the block for the fifth time, when the air quickened. He opened his eyes and discovered he was running—sprinting across the grass toward the door.

"How'd you know?" I adored this story, made him tell it all the time.

"God told me you were in trouble."

"Out loud? Did you hear Him?"

"Nope, not out loud. But He made me run, Reuben. I guess I figured it out on the way." . . .

When Dad skidded into the room, Dr. Nokes was sitting on the side of the bed holding my mother's hand. She was wailing. . . .

I was lying uncovered on a metal table across the room.

Dad lifted me gently. I was very clean from all that rubbing, and I was gray and beginning to cool. A little clay boy is what I was.

"Breathe," Dad said.

I lay in his arms. . . .

Dad leaned down, laid me back on the table, took off his jacket and wrapped me in it—a black canvas jacket with a quilted lining. I have it still. He left my face uncovered. . . .

As Mother cried out, Dad turned back to me, a clay child wrapped in a canvas coat, and said in a normal voice, "Reuben Land, in the name of the living God I am telling you to breathe."

THINK

"I took all this in and thought it through, inside and out." (Ecclesiastes 9:1)

- Wow! This passage definitely represents things that are true, noble, reputable, authentic, compelling, and gracious. Fill your mind with it one more time.
- What words or phrases in Enger's writing remind you of celebration? Explain.

PRAY

Slowly read the following poem a couple of times. What speaks to you? Ask God to bring a word or phrase to the surface. Then allow that word or phrase to begin your prayer. It might seem awkward at first. Fine, let it be awkward. But stick with it.

Loaves and Fishes

This is not
the age of information.
This is *not*
the age of information.
Forget the news,
and the radio,
and the blurred screen.
This is the time
of loaves
and fishes.
People are hungry,
and one good word is bread
for a thousand.

— DAVID WHYTE[5]

LIVE

These words from Whyte serve as a reminder of this section's theme—*celebration*:

> People are hungry,
> and one good word is bread
> for a thousand.

You've read from the journal entries, letters, and poems of others. Now it's your turn. What does God want you to live when it comes to *celebration*? Use the space below to write a letter to yourself. You might want to date the letter so you can reflect later where you were and what was going on in your life regarding *celebration*.

Date _____

Dear _____

NO RULES, JUST WRITE

"Receive and experience the amazing grace of the Master, Jesus Christ, deep, deep within yourselves."

(PHILIPPIANS 4:23)

Before You Begin

Take just a few moments to still your heart and mind. Remember, God desires to speak to *you* in these moments.

Stay with GOD!
Take heart. Don't quit.
I'll say it again:
Stay with GOD.

PSALM 27:14

READ

Philippians 4:15-23

You Philippians well know, and you can be sure I'll never forget it, that when I first left Macedonia province, venturing out with the Message, not one church helped out in the give-and-take of this work except you. You were the only one. Even while I was in Thessalonica, you helped out—and not only once, but twice. Not that I'm looking for handouts, but I do want you to experience the blessing that issues from generosity.

And now I have it all—and keep getting more! The gifts you sent with Epaphroditus were more than enough, like a sweet-smelling sacrifice roasting on the altar, filling the air with fragrance, pleasing God no end. You can be sure that God will take care of everything you need, his generosity exceeding even yours in the glory that pours from Jesus. Our God and Father abounds in glory that just pours out into eternity. Yes.

Give our regards to every follower of Jesus you meet. Our friends here say hello. All the Christians here, especially the believers who work in the palace of Caesar, want to be remembered to you.

Receive and experience the amazing grace of the Master, Jesus Christ, deep, deep within yourselves.

\ \ \ \

You've walked through Paul's letter to the Philippians. You've also walked through journal entries, letters, and poems from other pilgrims along the way. Now it's your turn. The challenge before you is to write three letters to three friends. These could include your spouse, an uncle you haven't spoken to for years, a former teacher, or your best friend from grade school. Go back through the lessons and allow God's Spirit to remind you of particularly meaningful places in Philippians, journal entries that resonated with you, or poems that touched you deeply. Then allow time for the faces of those family or friends to surface alongside those words.

Give this some time. If you build the space, they will come.

Just a side note: You don't have to limit your recipients to those who are living. You might write a letter to a grandparent who passed away or a soldier who died in harm's way. At times, writing to those who have gone on can open the door to significant growth and healing in our lives.

Then sit down with paper and pencil, or keyboard and screen, and share some of the thoughts and feelings that come to the surface. This might seem to be an unorthodox way to finish. But remember, this isn't a Bible study. The letters you send carry the possibility of witness, a way to invite soulfulness in a soul-less world. May they prompt reflection in another heart, honor the always-appropriate gift of memory, and speak truths of the past into today and eternity.

\ \ \ \

As you begin your letters (but end this book), ground your intentions by filling in three names.

Dear _____.

Dear _____.

Dear _____.

NOTES

LETTER 1: **FRIENDS**

1. Ralph Waldo Emerson, *Essays: First and Second Series* (New York: A. L. Burt Company, n.d.), 146–148.
2. Thomas Moore, *Soul Mates: Honoring the Mysteries of Love and Relationship* (New York: HarperPerennial, 1994), 93–94.
3. John Irving, *A Prayer for Owen Meany: A Novel* (New York: Ballantine Books, 1989), 1–2.
4. John Eldredge, *Wild at Heart: Discovering the Passionate Soul of a Man* (Nashville: Nelson, 2001), 174–175.
5. Ranier Maria Rilke, in David Whyte, *River Flow: New and Selected Poems 1984–2007* (Langley, WA: Many Rivers Press, 2007), 154. Printed with permission from Many Rivers Press, Langley, Washington. www.davidwhyte.com.

LETTER 2: **PRAYER**

1. Michael Yaconelli, *Messy Spirituality: God's Annoying Love for Imperfect People* (Grand Rapids, MI: Zondervan, 2002), 31.
2. Flannery O' Connor, *A Good Man Is Hard to Find and Other Stories* (New York: Harvest HBJ Book, 1955), 190–191.
3. Barbara Brown Taylor, *Leaving Church: A Memoir of Faith* (New York: HarperSanFrancisco, 2006), 68.
4. Ed Douglas, "Over the Top," *Outside*, September 2006, 72.
5. *House of Light* by Mary Oliver. Copyright © 1990 by Mary Oliver. Reprinted by permission of Beacon Press, Boston.

LETTER 3: **PROCLAMATION**

1. Wes Roberts and Glenn Marshall, *Reclaiming God's Original Intent for the Church* (Colorado Springs, CO: NavPress, 2004), 147–148.
2. Harry Middleton, *The Earth Is Enough: Growing Up in a World of Flyfishing, Trout, and Old Men* (Boulder, CO: Pruett Publishing, 1996), 158–159.
3. David James Duncan, *The River Why* (New York: Sierra Club Books, 1983), 41.
4. Walter Wangerin Jr., *The Orphean Passages: The Drama of Faith* (Grand Rapids, MI: Zondervan, 1986), 79–80.
5. T. S. Eliott, "Ash Wednesday," in *Collected Poems 1909–1962* (London: Faber and Faber Ltd., 1962).

LETTER 4: **SUFFERING**

1. Sue Monk Kidd, *When the Heart Waits: Spiritual Direction for Life's Sacred Questions* (New York: HarperCollins, 1990), 88.
2. Nicholas Wolterstorff, *Lament for a Son* (Grand Rapids, MI: Eerdmans, 1987), 96–97.
3. Excerpt from *The Lives of Rocks: Stories* by Rick Bass, 74–75. Copyright © 2006 by Rick Bass. Reprinted by permission of Houghton Mifflin Company. All rights reserved.
4. Gretel Ehrlich, *The Solace of Open Spaces* (New York: Penguin Books, 1985), 42–43.
5. Roy Daniells, "Noah," in Garrison Keillor, comp., *Good Poems* (New York: Penguin Books, 2002), 90. Permission pending.

LETTER 5: **ONE ANOTHER**

1. Jean Vanier, *Community and Growth* (New York: Paulist, 1989), 25.
2. Reprinted with the permission of Simon & Schuster Adult Publishing Group from *The Different Drum* by M. Scott Peck. Copyright © 1987 by M. Scott Peck, MD, PC.
3. William H. Willimon and Stanley Hauerwas, *Lord, Teach Us: The Lord's Prayer and the Christian Life* (Nashville: Abingdon, 1996), 65–66.

4. Henri J. M. Nouwen, *In the Name of Jesus: Reflections on Christian Leadership* (New York: Crossroad, 1989), 46–48.
5. Matthew 6:9-13.

LETTER 6: **THE WORLD**

1. Thomas Merton, *The Wisdom of the Desert: Sayings from the Desert Fathers of the Fourth Century* (New York: New Directions, 1970), 3–5.
2. Thomas Merton, *New Seeds of Contemplation* (New York: New Directions, 1972), 52–53.
3. Walter Capps, *The Monastic Impulse* (New York: Crossroad, 1983), 1–3.
4. Thomas Moore, *Meditations: On the Monk Who Dwells in Daily Life* (New York: HarperCollins, 1994), 33.
5. "I Praise," by Ranier Maria Rilke, translated by Denise Levertov, from *Light Up the Cave*, 98–99. Copyright © 1981 by New Directions Publishing Corp. Reprinted by permission of New Directions Publishing Corp.

LETTER 7: **JOY**

1. Ruth and Warren Myers, *31 Days of Praise* (Sisters, OR: Multnomah, 1994), 84.
2. Elisabeth Elliot, *Twelve Baskets of Crumbs* (Nashville: Abingdon, 1976), 49.
3. Rick Bass, *Winter: Notes from Montana* (New York: Mariner Books, 1991), 20.
4. Barry Lopez, *Resistance* (New York: Knopf, 2004), 11-12.
5. Gerald Stern, in Bill Moyers, *The Language of Life: A Festival of Poets*, ed. James Haba (New York: Doubleday, 1995), 382.

LETTER 8: **APPEARANCES**

1. Brennan Manning, *The Relentless Tenderness of Jesus* (Grand Rapids, MI: Revell, 2004), 47.
2. Wendell Berry, *The Memory of Old Jack* (New York: Counter Point Press, 1974), 181–182. Permission pending.

3. Excerpt from *The Lives of Rocks: Stories* by Rick Bass, 68–69. Copyright © 2006 by Rick Bass. Reprinted by permission of Houghton Mifflin Company. All rights reserved.

4. Ken Gire, *The Divine Embrace* (Wheaton, IL: Tyndale, 2003), 52–54.

5. Cleland B. McAfee, "Near to the Heart of God," *The Baptist Hymnal* (Nashville: Convention Press, 1991), 295.

LETTER 9: **GRACE**

1. Robert Farrar Capon, *Between Noon and Three: Romance, Law, and the Outrage of Grace* (Grand Rapids, MI: Eerdmans, 1997), 148–149.

2. Brennan Manning, *Abba's Child: The Cry of the Heart for Intimate Belonging* (Colorado Springs, CO: NavPress, 1994), 99.

3. Michael Yaconelli, *Dangerous Wonder: The Adventure of Childlike Faith* (Colorado Springs, CO: NavPress, 2003), 24–25.

4. G. K. Chesterton, *Orthodoxy: The Romance of Faith* (New York: Image Books, 1959), 120.

5. *The Cloud of Unknowing and the Book of Privy Counseling*, trans. William Johnston (New York: Doubleday, 1973), 60. Permission pending.

LETTER 10: **FOCUS**

1. Madeleine L'Engle, *Walking on Water: Reflections on Faith and Art* (Wheaton, IL: Harold Shaw Publishers, 1980), 53–54.

2. John Eldredge, *Waking the Dead: The Glory of a Heart Fully Alive* (Nashville: Nelson, 2003), 25–26.

3. Walter Wangerin Jr., *Ragman and Other Cries of Faith* (New York: HarperSanFrancisco, 1984), 75–76.

4. Bill Moyers, *The Language of Life: A Festival of Poets*, ed. James Haba (New York: Doubleday, 1995), 164.

5. Li-Young Lee, "I Ask My Mother to Sing" from *Rose*. Copyright © 1986 by Li-Young Lee. Reprinted with the permission of BOA Editions, Ltd. www.boaeditions.org.

LETTER 11: **CELEBRATION**

1. Rick Bass, *The Book of Yaak* (New York: Mariner Books, 1996), 38–40.
2. Sam Keen, *Fire in the Belly: On Being a Man* (New York: Bantam Books, 1991), 161–162.
3. Norman Maclean, *A River Runs Through It* (Chicago: University of Chicago Press, 1979), 61–64.
4. Lief Enger, *Peace Like a River* (New York: Grove Press, 2001), 1–3.
5. David Whyte, *River Flow: New and Selected Poems 1984–2007* (Langley, WA: Many Rivers Press, 2007), 358. Printed with permission from Many Rivers Press, Langley, Washington. www.davidwhyte.com.

CHECK OUT THESE OTHER GREAT TITLES FROM THE LIVING THE LETTERS SERIES!

In a modern world filled with disposable e-mails, receiving a handwritten letter remains one of life's simple pleasures. Rediscover the power of the written word through Paul's insightful letters.

Living the Letters: Galatians
The Navigators
978-1-60006-029-8
1-60006-029-3

Explore the rich wisdom of Galatians on topics such as spiritual discernment, intimacy with God, and our freedom in Christ.

Living the Letters: Ephesians
The Navigators
978-1-60006-030-4
1-60006-030-7

Paul writes to the Ephesians about finding your identity in Christ, experiencing the fullness of God, and living with faithful abandon.

Living the Letters: Colossians
The Navigators
978-1-60006-162-2
1-60006-162-1

Learn from the church of Colossae as Paul teaches them about suffering, grace, and prayer.